From Hogs to Heaven

Also by Tory Anderson

The Adventures of a Common Man: The Life of Rodney Anderson

From Hogs to Heaven

The Life of Laurel Rae Dickinson

Tory C Anderson

iUniverse, Inc.
Bloomington

From Hogs to Heaven
The Life of Laurel Rae Dickinson

iUniverse books may be ordered through booksellers or by contacting:

iUniverse
1663 Liberty Drive
Bloomington, IN 47403
www.iuniverse.com
1-800-Authors (1-800-288-4677)

ISBN: 978-1-4620-4303-3 (sc)
ISBN: 978-1-4620-4304-0 (ebk)

Printed in the United States of America

iUniverse rev. date: 08/09/2011

To my five T's who filled my life.

CONTENTS

Chapter 1: Where It All Began

Iowa is not a state of great fame among all the states of America. Except for those who attend grade school there and learn Iowa state history there aren't many who can tell you anything about Iowa. What famous events took place there? Didn't Abraham Lincoln start there? No, wait, that was Illinois. There is Des Moines. Everyone wants to visit Des Moines before they die. Well, maybe not. If you ask somebody what they know about Iowa they might be able to answer with a question, "Don't they grow a lot of corn in Iowa?" Beyond that Iowa is an obscure Central State that doesn't have much to excite the imagination—unless you grew up there. I grew up there.

If Iowa isn't obscure enough take a place in Iowa like Wilton Junction (later shortened to just Wilton). It's a crossroads in the country outside of Lime City. Still need a little help? Lime City is down the road from Muscatine. You've not heard of Muscatine either? You won't have too much trouble finding it. Muscatine is on the Mississippi River which makes up the eastern border of Iowa. In 1933, during the dusty depression, a few miles outside of Wilton Junction there sat a big, red barn with the great big fading words, "Burr Oak Grove Stock Farm" written across it. Near the barn was a two-story house. On March 14th of that same year I was born in that house. The barn and the house are gone now. Nowadays people pass by on the road and probably don't even look out their window. For me the location is a solar flare in my memory and imagination.

Although my life ended up in quite a different place my life began in a bedroom in that Iowa farmhouse. Each room of that house is still solid and strong in my memory. I don't know who built that house, but whoever built it built it to last. As far as my family history goes I know that it belonged to my Grandma Dickinson. My father eventually bought it from her. Then my sister Marge and her husband bought it from him and raised their children there, so the house stayed in the family for four generations. It stood tall and strong throughout decades of sticky Iowa summers and frigid Iowa winters. After Marge and her husband sold the house it quickly passed into ruin, eventually burned and the remains torn down. It was as if it lost its will to live when the family left.

Compared to today's houses my farmhouse was simple. The main floor consisted of four rooms: a living room, a dining room, my parent's bedroom, and the kitchen. The kitchen was the room where most of the living went on. For many years it contained a wood stove we used for cooking and for heat. There was a sink with a pump on either end. Both ran only cold water. One pump was for drinking and the other was for washing dishes. We had to heat all of our hot water on the stove. In addition to our wood stove there was a pot bellied stove in the dining room. The wood stove and pot bellied stove were our only source of heat in the house. The stoves did just fine for the main floor, but my two sisters and I slept upstairs and not much heat ever made it that far during those cold Iowa winters. We made up for the lack of heat with lots of blankets and feather beds. Upstairs consisted of a hallway with four bedrooms, two on the west end and two on the east end. Marjorie, my oldest sister slept in one of the west rooms. Dorothy, my next oldest sister, slept with me in the other west room. One of the bedrooms at the east end of the hall was used for guests or for the hired man when we had one. The other bedroom was closed to us children. It was my Grandma Dickinson's room when she came to visit us. My sisters and I were forbidden to enter it.

In addition to the four bedroom doors there was one more door in that hallway. It opened to a narrow stairway that led to the attic. The attic was an exciting and frightful place for me. I was always afraid that somehow the door would close behind me when I went up and I would be trapped up there. It was beastly hot there in the summer. Light came in through windows at either end of the attic and you could easily make your way around the "stuff" that was stored up there. Flies always found there way to the attic and buzzed at the windows trying to get out. I would look out these windows and get dizzy at being so high from the ground.

The house wasn't built with a cellar, but my Dad built one. I understand it took quite some time. He did it all with a hand shovel.

My sister Marjorie remembers Dad passing buckets of dirt outside where she would load it into her little wagon. She would pull it to where she was piling the dirt and dump it there. The cellar turned out to be quite large. One entry to the cellar was through the back door which was in an enclosed porch. It led to the part of the cellar where we did the washing. We had an old washer down there—the kind that had roller ringers that would squeeze the water out of the clothes. We had to heat water on the stove upstairs and carry it down to the washer. We didn't have to carry the dirty water back up after the washing was done. Dad had put a drain in the cellar floor and we emptied the water into that. The other half of the cellar had shelves and was where Mom put all of the vegetables and fruits she canned every year. There was an entrance to this part of the cellar from the kitchen. One other entrance to this part of the cellar was a wide cellar door that opened directly outside. Through these doors Dad brought the potatoes, corn, and other vegetables that we stored in bins for the winter. In between the two parts of the cellar was a toilet that didn't always flush. We would have to pour water down it. Off to one side of the cellar was a room where Dad would keep the coal for the furnace we later put in. The outside wall was slanted and made of rocks. Like the attic this room scared me. I just knew that the rock wall would fall in on me.

My dad was a farmer. Our house was a farm house. We lived out in the country on the farm. I suppose all this means that I grew up as a farm girl. To those who know me today this information might confuse them or at least make them smile. Since my youth I have become a city girl and enjoy all the conveniences that a city brings. Anymore I don't like being too far from a Costco or a fast food restaurant. Still, it is true that I grew up the daughter of an old fashioned farmer on an old fashioned farm. By "old fashioned farm" I mean "family farm." My family lived off the crops and livestock my dad produced on that farm.

On those old fashioned farms it was customary for farmers to have large families with several boys who could help with the farm work. Unfortunately for my Dad, he and my mother were only able to have three children—all of them girls. I don't recall Dad ever expressing disappointment that he had girls instead of boys, but I

3

wonder if there was a flicker of disappointment in his mind when he was told that I, his third and probably last child, was a girl. But Dad wasn't one to waste time on what he wished for. Instead, he took his girls and got busy farming. Each of us girls was born approximately five years apart. Marjorie was about as good on a farm as any boy could have been. She was strong in body and spirit and could drive a tractor as well as command the work horses. Dorothy wasn't far behind Marjorie in farming ability. I, on the other hand, didn't make a very good "farm son."

For several years while I was growing up we used horses and a mule to do a lot of the farm work. The horses didn't make a very good team. Their names were Babe and Bob. Babe was lazy and bellicose while Bob was spirited and ready to go. Dad would grow large fields of corn to use later as feed for the animals. When it was time to harvest the corn he had combines to do the work, but before he could use them effectively he had to clear a strip of corn away from the fence. He would do this manually by walking through this strip of corn stalks and tearing the ears of corn off the stalks and tossing them over the fence into a wagon that was keeping pace with him. When I was old enough I became the unhappy operator of that wagon. The horses that did as they were told by my two older sisters gave me fits. They sensed my lack of command and took full advantage of it. Dad wanted to be able to walk along as quickly as possible tossing the corn against the high sideboard on the wagon that caused the ears to fall into the wagon, but as I struggled with the horses I would sometimes be too far ahead and often too far behind breaking Dad's rhythm. This would make him unhappy and cause me a little stress.

We also had a mule named Jude. Jude did various jobs around the farm, but the one where we had to work together was harvesting hay. This was long before the days of automatic bailers and stackers. When I was younger I remember men walking beside the horse drawn wagon pitching hay into the wagon with pitch forks. Eventually we got a machine that put the hay into the wagon automatically. After the wagon was full we had to put the loose hay into the barn up in the "mow." The mow was a loft where the hay could be kept dry and where it was easy to throw hay down to feed the animals. The wagon would pull up near the barn where there was a rope fed through a pulley up high. On one end of the rope was a big double fork that would be shoved into the hay so that it could be lifted. On the other end of the rope was Jude and supposedly in command of Jude was me. When the fork was in the hay I was to make Jude begin pulling until the hay was in position in the mow where Dad would trip the fork and unload the hay. As with the horses I had no sense of command. Jude had no love for pulling those heavy loads of hay and would often ignore my words of encouragement and stop pulling before the hay had reached the mow. Dad would holler at me for letting Jude get away such behavior. I wanted to do better like my sisters did before me, but I was just different. My dad only struck me once while I was growing up and that was a swat on the bottom when he was frustrated that I couldn't control Jude better.

For the longest time I never did understand the difference between a hay stack and a straw stack. One day while I was out and about the farm I noticed a newborn calf lying by the hay stack. When I went to the house and told Dad he had me come along with him on the tractor to go get the calf. Since I had told him the calf was by the haystack Dad drove out into the field where the haystack was. It was then I realized I had told him the wrong stack. I cut my losses by tapping him on the shoulder and telling him that the calf was actually by the "other" stack. No harm had been done, but he expressed his disappointment that I didn't know a haystack from a straw stack.

I may not have been the tomboy my sisters were and not the best farm hand, but in spite of that, or maybe because of that, I had a great love of the farm. The animals form a large part of my good memories. Along with chickens we had ducks. Each morning after Mom let them out of their pen they would run as fast as they could all the way around the house quacking all the way before they would return to the pen and the food Mom had thrown out for them. No one ever could explain to me why they did this. It must have been the joy of their daily freedom. It was good they enjoyed their freedom when they had it because each one would eventually be eaten for dinner.

We had cows, some for milking and some for meat. Dorothy and I were tasked with the milking. Getting into the barn to do the milking was easy in the winter. The barnyard, full of slimy cow manure and mud, would be frozen and we could walk right over it.

In the warmer months, however, I remember donning my galoshes and working my way through the muck. The green slime would almost spill over the top of my galoshes at times and often my feet would become stuck in the sticky suction. Dad would remedy this by scooping up the manure with his tractor and loading it into the manure wagon. He would then spread it over the fields for fertilizer. Fertilizing days were particularly smelly.

While milking the cows Dorothy and I would try to recreate the rhythms of the popular songs of the day that we heard on the radio by squirting streams of milk against the side of the bucket. It was surprising how often we could guess the tune that each other was playing. During the evening milkings, when it was growing dark, I would look out the barn window as I milked and watch an airport beacon go round. It was a green light that would grow steadily brighter as it turned towards me and then dim as it turned away. I never visited that airport and to this day I don't know what it was called, but the light pulsing away in the distance almost hypnotized me. I suppose it put me into a reflective mood wondering what my place on Earth was and what my future had in store for me. In the medical field describing pain can be important. Many times in my life, when I have needed to describe pain I was feeling I would use that pulsing light as a metaphor for my pain.

Dorothy, or Dorty as I called her, was five years older than me and Marge five years older than her. Both sisters were gone from home long before I was out of school. This left me to do all of the farm work that they used to do. In the summers the cows would be let out of the barn each morning. They would saunter down a long lane between two fields to reach their daytime pasture. In the afternoons I would walk up this lane to reach the cows and bring them in. I often plodded down the lane barefoot in the dust. I always sang as I went. Uncle Elwood, whose farm bordered our farm told me once that he would always hear me singing and know that it was also time to milk his cows. Our cows would often be laying under a tree resting in the shade. Sometimes, when they saw me coming, they would get up and meet me on their way back to the barn. After their rest and with their stomachs full of pasture grass they would let cow pies splat on the ground behind them. If I was daydreaming or too lost in song I wouldn't notice and step in the warm, slimy paddies. That's a feeling you don't want to have between your toes. The cows would enter the barn, get a drink of water, and then each find her own stall. I would lock their heads in place where they could eat their oats, but not back out while I was milking. There would always be three or four gallons of milk. I would take the milk down to the cellar and put it in the separator where the milk would be separated from the cream. The separator had many blades that made cleaning it difficult. It was nice having fresh milk and cream, though.

We had a sixty foot windmill in our yard near the house. It pumped our drinking water out of the well. There was a ladder that went nearly to the top ending at a small platform where you could stand. Marge would climb to the top all the time. I never dared to go all the way up. I did like watching the big blades spinning in the wind. Sometimes, when the wind was strong, I worried that the windmill would fall over on me or the house.

We had a double clothesline tied from the house to the windmill. Mom would bring the wash from the washing machine in the cellar and hang it out on the line. The lines were mainly for the sheets and linens. The overalls Mom would just drape over the fence. When I was little I would take a pad of paper and a pencil with me and stand in front of the clothes on the line and pretend they were products in my store that I was selling. My name was always Ann Evans and I would write down my imaginary customers' orders on my paper. When the laundry was dry we would take the sheets and make the beds. I loved the way the beds smelled with the air dried sheets. As a married woman I was hanging sheets on a line when I had my first labor pains when pregnant with my first child, Tami.

With all of our cows, pigs, cats, dogs, chickens and ducks came babies. I loved baby anything except snakes. I tried to make pets out of everything. I would climb on the baby pigs when they got bigger and ride them until I fell off. Sometimes I would get to hand feed calves from bottles. I liked that. I always wanted to have a house cat to keep me company inside, but Mom would never allow it. I never lost hope that she would change her mind until once a cat snuck into the house unknown to the rest of us. It was on a Sunday and when we came home from church Mom immediate noticed the smell of cat poop. We searched all over and found that the cat had pooped deep under the couch. Mom was greatly displeased and I lost all hope of a house pet after that. I had a favorite dog named Old Shep. He was a great companion around the farm and very well behaved. He would never try to get through the garden gate before me, but would wait for me to go through first. We lost Old Shep the day Dad was dipping pigs in a chemical that would kill parasites on their skin. Old Shep would nip them when they came out of the dip to hurry them up. Apparently he ingested some of the poison because later that day he had convulsions and died. Even my stoic Dad felt bad about that. He felt he should have known better than to have Old Shep loose at the dipping.

Of course all animals end up dying on a farm. Their deaths made life better for the rest of us. I always felt bad when the day came to kill a pig or a cow, but not so bad that I ever became a vegetarian. The day we killed a pig or a cow was a busy day. Dad and the hands would shoot a pig and then hang it up and slit its throat to drain the blood. Mom would get the head and boil it to make head cheese. I never hung around long enough to see exactly how she did that. The men would take out the large intestines, clean it thoroughly, and then stuff spiced meat in it for sausage. The cuts of meat would be wrapped in wax paper and then sent off to a meat locker in Wilton and kept frozen there. When we made our weekly trip in to Wilton the meat locker was always the last stop to pick up the meat for the week.

The chickens weren't such a process, but they still took time. If company showed up unexpectedly for dinner Mom would run out the hen house with her long handled hook, hook a chicken's legs so she could grab it easier, and cut off its head. The chicken would flap its wings hard as it died splattering blood all over everything. Mom would then dip the dead hen in boiling water and then pluck it. After that she would light a wadded piece of newspaper on fire and use it to burn off all the pin feathers. Then came the gutting and cleaning. Finally she would cut up the chicken and fry it. All this work was for a "quick" dinner. Mom's chicken always tasted so good.

I helped feed the chickens. We fed them corn we had grown the season before. We had a corn grinder out by the corn cribs. I would put one ear at a time into the grinder, turn the crank and the shelled corn would spill into a bucket. I would carry two bucket loads of corn at a time to the chicken house. I don't know if my parents appreciated how hard I worked, but I know my Aunt Vella did. She once commented to my Mom, after seeing me carrying the heavy buckets, that I was going to ruin my back by carrying such heavy loads. I don't remember my loads being lessened after that, though.

We once lost a calf in a watering trough. It had fallen in and drowned. I felt horrible when I found it. Other cows were standing around including the drowned calf's mother. It was mooing mournfully. I swear I saw tears in the mama cow's eyes. The sow's weren't as caring about their babies. Dad would often have to kick and shove a sow to get her to move off a trapped and squealing piglet before the piglet was crushed. There was a patch of timber out back on our property. One evening a sow had wandered out there to make a place to have her babies. Dad didn't want her to have her babies out there. He grabbed his leather whip and called me to go with him to help him get the sow back to the barn. I wasn't happy about this, but I didn't have much of a choice. The sows were big and scary. When we found the sow she was lying in her nest. Dad told me to get on the other side of her to turn her toward the barn when she got up. He then cracked his whip encouraging the sow to get up. She got up all right and charged me. Dad deftly stung her with his whip and turned her before she got to me. I'm glad he did because it wouldn't have been pretty if she had reached me. As usual I hadn't been much help after all, but everything turned out fine.

From the picture I have painted so far it may appear that my Dad was all business and a stern fellow. The truth is, he was. He could very easily have stepped out of the picture, "American Gothic" showing the unsmiling farmer with his pitch fork standing next to his equally unsmiling wife. His life was the farm and there wasn't much room for anything else. I was his baby girl, but he never showed any sentiment towards me, at least not until he was in his nineties. He never took me for walks, or held my hand, or had long talks with me. I don't remember him ever offering me a hug. He certainly wasn't one to feel sorry for a person, or at least show that he felt sorry. In our used Model T we pulled up to a park one day. My dad took his pipe out of his mouth, held it out the open window and knocked it against the car door to remove the ashes. The breeze carried the ashes in through the back window into my eyes. I cried a little as I rubbed the ashes out of my eyes. I don't remember Dad apologizing, but I do remember Mom scolding him. On another occasion, when I was a bit older, I was going to the barn to do my bovine chores. I wore braces on my upper and lower teeth at this time. I ignored the gusty wind that was blowing and was singing as I reached the barn doors. As I pulled the barn door the wind caught it and smacked it into my face forcing the wires of my braces into my upper gums. I went screaming to the house with blood running down my face. Mom immediately put me in the car and we made an emergency trip to the dentist in Tipton. The dentist got me all straightened out. Mom felt bad for me, but Dad just shook his head that I would let such a silly thing happen to me.

Even so I never felt sorry for myself for having a Dad like mine. I didn't know Dad's could be any different and thought he was a proper Dad. Dad may have been all business, but he wasn't mean by any means. He was a responsible man and made sure that his farm was productive and his family well-taken-care-of. And we were well-taken-care-of. I don't remember ever wanting for anything I really needed in my life. This was how Dad showed his love for his family. As my own children grew up I saw him act much more tenderly with them. Near the end of his life, when he was living with me and Reed, he told me for the first time that he loved me. I could tell that he meant it.

Mom was the complete opposite of my Dad. While she worked hard and expected me to work hard also I can also remember her cuddling me in her lap when I was upset about something. She hummed me no-word songs until I felt better. She attended every one of my church and school functions. She more than made up for my Dad's lack of affection.

This is a picture of my farm home from the rear. I always thought this was the rear of the home but my mother told me it was actually the front of the home, facing the road. We always entered from the other side of the home, however.

My Dad and I are tending to the pigs around the big water tank. The hog house on the left, corn bin, and then the big cow barn on the right. Taken about 1940.

I had a brother-in-law in the Marines during World War 11 and I am standing on the hay stack giving a solute. However I am doing it with my left hand. Taken about 1940.

This is the first picture ever taken of me in 1935. My cousin Bill, in front, and I were in our old wagon. I was recovering from the measles and double mastoidectomy.

This picture I will always cherish, as it shows my home from the front, with the windmill and my first car that Dad bought me in 1953 when I finished nurses training. I always had a pet calf or pig and this shows my love for them. My car was a '49 Chevrolet.

These are my wonderful parents, Lloyd and Grace Dickinson, with a new car they purchased. Dad was more comfortable in overalls and a straw hat. My mother was an angel.

My mother and dad and my two sisters. Dorothy on the left and Marjorie on the right. I had just had my first baby in 1958 when this was taken.

Chapter 2: My Education

I'm certain that if someone from the future had dropped by my elementary school in 1938 and described the state of education in America today my classmates and I would have been both amazed and terrified. I'm thinking we would have been more terrified than amazed. Although there are many amazing aspects to public education today I'm afraid the descriptions of mass killings by fellow students, drugs, gangs, metal detectors, policemen in the hallways, alcohol, and pregnant children would have been overwhelming. Even though I started elementary school in 1938—well into the 20th century—my school experience had many of the idyllic elements of the 19th Century. That first day when Mom bundled me up against a frozen March morning and sent me to that one-room school house she, nor I, knew what wonderful things education had in store for me.

My elementary school was located in Lime City. Don't get any grand ideas about Lime City. The name suggests much more than the reality can bear out. Twelve miles south of Tipton and 10 miles north of Wilton someone found a large formation of limestone. They started a quarry to take advantage of this natural resource. It being too far to travel back and forth from Wilton or Tipton some houses were built for the quarry workers. There were only a few homes, but the workers had enough children that when the area farm children were added to their numbers it justified a school being built. I don't remember the number of children attending in one school year ever reaching more than sixteen. The size of the school building reflected this. There were only two rooms in this school. The one that served as the classroom had a big pot-bellied stove in it, black chalkboards on the walls, and our desks. The desks were of varied sizes to accommodate children who ranged in age from first grade through eighth grade. They were the kind of desks where the seats were attached to the desk. The top of the desk lifted and we put our books, crayons, and pencils inside. On the other side of the double doors in the wall at the front of the room was another room with a stage and used for our school productions and presentations. Thoughts of that little school house bring back warm feelings to me now. Recently I was able to visit Lime City again when I attended a funeral. Even though it has been over seventy years since I began school there the school house is still there. It is now a private home and in good shape.

School mornings began about 6:30 with my Mom calling up the stairs with a simple, "It's time to get up." There was no heat upstairs and so my room was cold. I liked school so much that even the chill didn't keep me in bed for long. I would pull on my clothes and run downstairs to stand by the cook stove to warm up. Mom would feed me oatmeal or eggs and bacon. She put bread on a long fork and toasted it over the coals. Often it arrived on my plate burned. After breakfast I would bundle up, take the sack lunch Mom handed me and then head out across the frozen fields. By the roads the school was a mile-and-a-half from my home. If I cut across the fields it was only a mile. In nicer weather the plowed fields were harder to walk across so I took the roads. The walk to and from school was a good time for singing, contemplation, and just day-dreaming. In the winter I made my way to and from school quickly because it was so cold. The pot bellied stove at school was a good friend of mine as it thawed my toes back to life. Once, on my way home, I climbed over fence and then started across the ice in the ditch on the other side. I fell through and soaked my legs. I hurried home where my sweet mother dried me off, held me on her lap while my legs warmed in the oven. My older sister, Dorothy, was five years ahead of me and so we went to that same school room for about three years. Sometimes we would ride a horse to school. Since she was older she would sit in front and I would get the more uncomfortable seat behind her. I couldn't see very well from behind Dorty and I didn't like the way sitting near the horses back end bounced me. One day, after school, I demanded that I get a turn to sit in front. I must have put up a fuss because Dorty gave in set me in front of her. This arrangement worked fine until the horse reached for some sweet grass beside the road. Dorty never admitted it, but I'm pretty sure she allowed the horse to lower its head for the grass knowing what would happen.

I slid forward down the horse's neck and landed in the grass. Dorty hadn't made any attempt to grab me. She just laughed as I pouted and ran the rest of the way home crying. To get on the horse we had to bring it along side some steps or something else that would get us closer to Bob's back. Since there was nothing nearby on the road that would serve that purpose Dort just shrugged and rode on without me. I walked the rest of the way thinking of how much I didn't like riding horses anyway.

Although there weren't that many children in the class, the varied ages kept the teacher busy. But she had her techniques that kept the class running smoothly. Some lessons she directed toward the entire class such as geography or maybe history. On other subjects she would call the various grades to the front one by one to go over times tables or science subjects. While she did this the rest of us would sit and study quietly at our desks. I remember only misbehaving one time. My mother started me in school after I turned 5 in March of 1938 even though it was half way through the school year. It was sometime soon after that I was chewing pieces of paper and spitting them at some of the other kids. My teacher happened to be my cousin, Paul Hain. He strode over to me and glared down at me without saying a word. Even compared to other grownups he was a tall man, but to me his 6' 3" frame made him a giant. I had to crane my neck to look up into his disapproving face. My school days of wild antics were over and I never needed reproving again. Generally all of us were well-behaved. Every once in a while a child, usually a boy, would find himself sitting on the chair in the corner in the front of the classroom. That was about as harsh as discipline got. When nature called we would raise our hand and hold up one finger or two. This was to give the teacher an idea of how long we might be gone. There was no need of a hall pass since there was no hall. The bathroom was an outhouse out back.

Since my two sisters were so much older than I was I grew up much like an only child. Since we had no near neighbors I walked to school alone. But I did often see a friend on the way. Her name was Jerry Daut and she was a farmer's wife. She lived in the farm house across the road from the school. I would make my way across the fields, over fences, through her barnyard, over her yard and then up her driveway across from the school. Sometimes on the coldest days she would call to me from her door as I was walking through her yard and invite me in. She would always fry me an egg and butter some toast for me. On days that are special in my memory now she would tell me she was going to ask my mother if I could stay the night. After school I would walk back up her driveway and anxiously look for the signal. If there was a magazine leaning against her window I knew I could stay. I loved staying at Jerry's house because it meant I got out of chores. But even better it was because the Daut's had a real indoor bathroom. The icing on the cake was the fact that Jerry would be making my lunch the next day. My mother always fed me well, but my sack lunches were usually the same thing day-after-day—a sandwich, maybe a cookie, and an apple. Jerry's lunches were always different and so seemed special. She often sent me with hot soup in a thermos. One day she sent me a dish of homemade ice cream. When I got to school I put it in a snowbank to keep it cold. At noon I ate the ice cream slowly and made sure that all the other kids saw me. I felt pretty special.

We put on many class presentations for our parents throughout elementary school. It was always exciting when our teacher would open up the double doors that led into the other room with the stage. I enjoyed exploring behind the stage and playing in the curtains. Our presentations followed the same plan. There would be a poetry reading or other recitation, then the dramatic presentation, then a musical number and it would be over. Our parents would come and sit in our desks to enjoy the entertainment. My mom never missed a presentation although Dad usually couldn't make it. One year I got to sing the "Star Spangled Banner" all by myself at a presentation. I loved to sing and I was very excited. The day before the presentation Teacher let me go into the other room and practice on the stage. I sang the song over and over again. Finally my teacher came in and kindly asked me to stop. I must have driven her crazy.

My elementary days went by without any extraordinary events and most of my memories are good, but there were the kids from this one family. It seemed like they had a child in every grade. I remember them being mean. You didn't want to catch their attention because they could make life at school hard. I remember sitting in the outhouse one day at recess while one of the girls taunted me through the door. In a sing-song voice she repeated, "Your little brother died. There was something wrong with your little brother." She was very cruel. Aside from that incident my school days were happy. We listened to music almost every day on a windup Victrola. I loved that. One day, while everyone was doing their own thing I was writing my alphabet on the blackboard and saying the sound of each letter out loud as I went. My friend, Mary Ann Trafton, was sitting in her desk behind me cleaning her glasses. I wrote the letter "H" on the board and said the "Huh" sound just as she made the same sound puffing air on her glasses. We couldn't stop giggling after that.

After I graduated from eighth grade my world suddenly expanded. It didn't expand much, but compared to the few fields and farm houses that had comprised my world for the first twelve years of my life, riding the bus into Tipton—a city—was exciting. Both of my sisters had gone to ninth grade in Wilton. I really don't know why my dad and mom sent me to Tipton instead. After ninth grade my parents must have changed their minds because they sent me the other direction to Wilton for the rest of high school.

In high school my life expanded even more. In addition to the daily ride into the city I became involved in many extracurricular activities that took me to many different cities. Although I felt like I was tall, ugly, and unpopular I had a lot of fun in high school. I was in the school plays. I took up the clarinet and played in the band and orchestra. Each year I went to competitions and won awards for vocal solos and duets. My love for singing had not decreased from elementary school. I sang in the girls chorus, the mixed chorus, a trio, a sextet, and I sang solos. As with the clarinet I went to competition for singing also. I can remember arriving back in Wilton after one of these competitions where my mother was waiting to take me home. I ran to her proclaiming that I had gotten a superior. My mother was always so supportive. For one of our Christmas programs I was asked to sing "Silent Night" in French. I probably didn't do the French Language any honor, but it was an honor for me to be asked to sing a solo and it sounded beautiful, at least to my ears.

Sports became a part of my life in high school also although I never participated directly. I joined the team by becoming the statistician. I would sit to the side of the team, usually behind a table, and keep track of points and fouls and things. It was exciting participating in this way and made me feel a part of Wilton High even if I wasn't one of the popular crowd. At one basketball game our team was sitting up on the stage and I with them. At half time the team went into the locker room. I was left on the stage alone to finish up the first half statistics. I heard the kids from my school giving a cheer. I looked up wondering why they were cheering when the team was gone to find that they were aiming the cheer at me. I don't know whose idea that cheer was, but I was surprised and flattered.

The coach raised my self-esteem by making me feel really needed. Because I lived so far away from the city on a farm it made it difficult to make it to games. The games wouldn't start for several hours after school, but I lived too far away to be able to go home and come back. The coach suggested that I stay at his home with him and his wife on game nights. This worked out very well and made game days all the more exciting. My sisters didn't participate much in extracurricular activities. After school they would go back home and do the farm work. For some reason Dad didn't seem to mind my extracurricular activities even though he had to do my after-school chores. Perhaps this was his way of showing me he loved me. He could have easily forbade me the extracurricular activities and demanded that I fulfill my household duties. Instead, he let me loose and I'll always love him for it.

I was as interested in boys as any other typical girl and daydreamed of love. I was always jealous when I saw other girls holding hands with a boy. When I was younger my Grandma Dickinson had introduced me to one of her neighbors as her "Ugly string bean of a granddaughter." That had hurt me deeply and I never forgot it. I was tall and skinny and went through high school feeling ugly. During my junior year a boy befriended me. We actually went steady for the year. He took me to the junior prom. That was my first formal dance. I didn't know how to dance and it was awkward at first, but turned out all right. We wrote letters to each other all summer, but when our senior year started he broke up with me. I was heartbroken at first. Luckily young hearts heal quickly and I went on to have a fine senior year. I did end up going to the senior prom alone, but there were many other girls there without dates also and we managed to enjoy ourselves.

Throughout high school I had never given much thought to what I would do after I graduated. Marge had gotten married soon after graduation. Dort had taken a job in a bank. As a senior, with the help of my dad, I had gotten a job as a book keeper at a little store in town. I found the responsibility of book keeping enjoyable and thought that book keeping would be my calling after I graduated. As graduation neared there was talk of college and scholarships, but I didn't pay any attention. People from various schools and organizations came to speak with us and recruit us to their cause. One organization was the American Cancer Society. They said they were awarding scholarships to the winners of an essay contest. The theme was "Why I want to be a nurse." I had never thought of becoming a nurse and their presentation didn't hold any interest for me, but writing the essay did. I wrote the essay only because we were asked to do it—not because of any desire to win. Little did I know that in writing that essay I opened a door that had a profound effect upon my life.

It is strange how we often place great importance upon things that have very little weight in our life. For instance, when my junior year boy friend broke up with me it seemed like the rest of my life would be in black and white. I thought I would never be happy again. Now I can hardly remember that boy's name. On the other hand, while writing that essay where I was just making up reasons why I wanted to be a nurse, I thought I was doing nothing more than another writing exercise. In the end it was that ordinary, dull writing exercise that so richly colored the rest of my life.

Three weeks after I turned in my essay a letter arrived for me. I had forgotten all about my essay by then and had no idea what this letter could be about. When I opened the letter and read that the National Cancer Society was offering me a full-ride scholarship to train as a nurse I was speechless. Being offered a full-ride scholarship was a great honor, but the idea of being a nurse was foreign to me. I had never considered it one way or the other. Excited and with shaking hands I showed Mom the letter and asked, "Should I be a nurse?" Her answer came without thought, "Of course you should." With her support my decision was made and I never looked back.

I graduated from high school shortly before starting nurses training. I clearly remember that afternoon in May of 1950. I had turned 17 only two months before in March. For the first time I donned high heels. I can't remember who I borrowed them from, but they were too small and hurt my feet. I proudly walked up the aisle and took my place with the other seniors on the stand. I can't remember much of what was said at graduation, but I do remember singing my solo, "I Love Life." When the graduation ceremony ended I walked out into a new life that the scholarship made possible.

Just eight weeks later, in August, I left the farming life forever. I loaded a couple of suitcases into the 1949 Chevrolet and Mom and Dad drove me to the nurses' dormitory at St. Luke's hospital in Davenport, Iowa. They returned to the farm—my old world—and I, a little nervous, stepped into the new. I didn't remain nervous for long. In fact, as my studies began I found myself remarkably at home. I was only seventeen while all the other first-years were at least eighteen. I was a little bit proud of that. Almost every day, for the next six months, I drove a station wagon full of girls across the Mississippi River to Rock Island, Illinois. All of our classes were held there in Augustana College. In those six months we took a year's worth of classes in anatomy, physiology, psychology, and other subjects. It wasn't easy. When we weren't in classes we were training at St Luke's hospital in giving bed baths, checking blood pressure, taking temperature and all other sorts of patient care.

After only six weeks we were put to work on the hospital floor. I loved my student nurses uniform—blue-striped dress, white hose, and white nurses shoes. Our dresses were starched so much they were almost as stiff as cardboard. I didn't mind as it just made me feel more important. There was a system of stripes that we wore on the nurses' cap that indicated what year we were in our training. I was proud each time I added another stripe. We student nurses worked all shifts and on all floors. At times I felt as if we ran the hospital.

During those three years of training we each spent three months at a psychiatric hospital in Independence, Iowa, and then three months doing pediatric training at a large children's hospital in Cincinnati, Ohio. During our senior year we were allowed to work for three months in a medical area of our choice. I chose surgery. My love for surgery I attribute to the Director of Surgery. She trained me so thoroughly and I felt like I was her 'star' pupil. It turned out

I chose well for myself as I really enjoyed the surgical atmosphere. Although I wasn't the one performing the life or death procedures on the patient, I was important in helping the surgeon arrive at a successful conclusion to each surgery. The surgeons liked how I could anticipate what they needed and firmly place the needed tools into their hands.

During my surgical training I caught the eye of Dr. Goldstein. He was neurosurgeon. I assisted in a couple of his surgeries quite coincidentally. I just happened to be assigned to work his surgery on days that he operated. After assisting him on these surgeries he started requesting me to be his assisting nurse on all of his surgeries. He liked me so much that he offered me a job as his full-time assistant after I graduated. I was so proud to have a job offer before I had even graduated. My parents were proud to. I would come home and excitedly tell them all about my experiences. It wasn't surprising when Mom expressed her pride in me, but it was when my usually stoic father started lighting up when he listened to me. Often he would say, "Now, come on down off the third floor. We live on the first floor here." He pretended to act as if he were chiding me for acting as if I were now superior to him and Mom, but there was a smile in his voice and pride in his eyes.

In September of 1953 I graduated from the nursing program at St. Luke's hospital. Graduating from high school was a nice experience but graduating as a nurse was one of the greatest achievements of my life. Walking down the aisle in a totally white uniform with the graduate cap on my head, I felt like I had 'made it'. My Mom and Dad both attended my graduation and I knew then that writing that essay on why I wanted to be a nurse was a divine intervention in my life. I loved being a nurse, and I know that is one reason my dad chose to come live his remaining days with me.

Although my formal schooling ended at that graduation my medical education continued until the day I retired 41 years later in 1994. When I look back at the humble beginnings of my education in that two room school house and then forward to the surgeries I assisted in and the emergency departments I ran I find myself grateful for the education I was allowed to have. My parents' education was basic, but it was enough to allow them a satisfying life. They were highly educated in the heart as was shown when they let me leave their world—even encouraged me to leave—to further my education when the opportunity arose. I am proud of my children for taking advantage of educational opportunities that have come along in their lives. Four of the five have gone on to earn degrees in higher education and the fifth, although having no official degree, speaks four languages and works for the government. But more importantly they have educated hearts which have led to fulfilling lives. The fifth child mentioned above, at age 50, is now a full time college student, after completing his 22 years of military service. I am proud.

My first school picture. Mother made the dress I was wearing and I loved it as it had a velvet collar. Taken in 1938.

Wilton High School, where I graduated in 1950. A new high school is now in use and this is an elementary school.

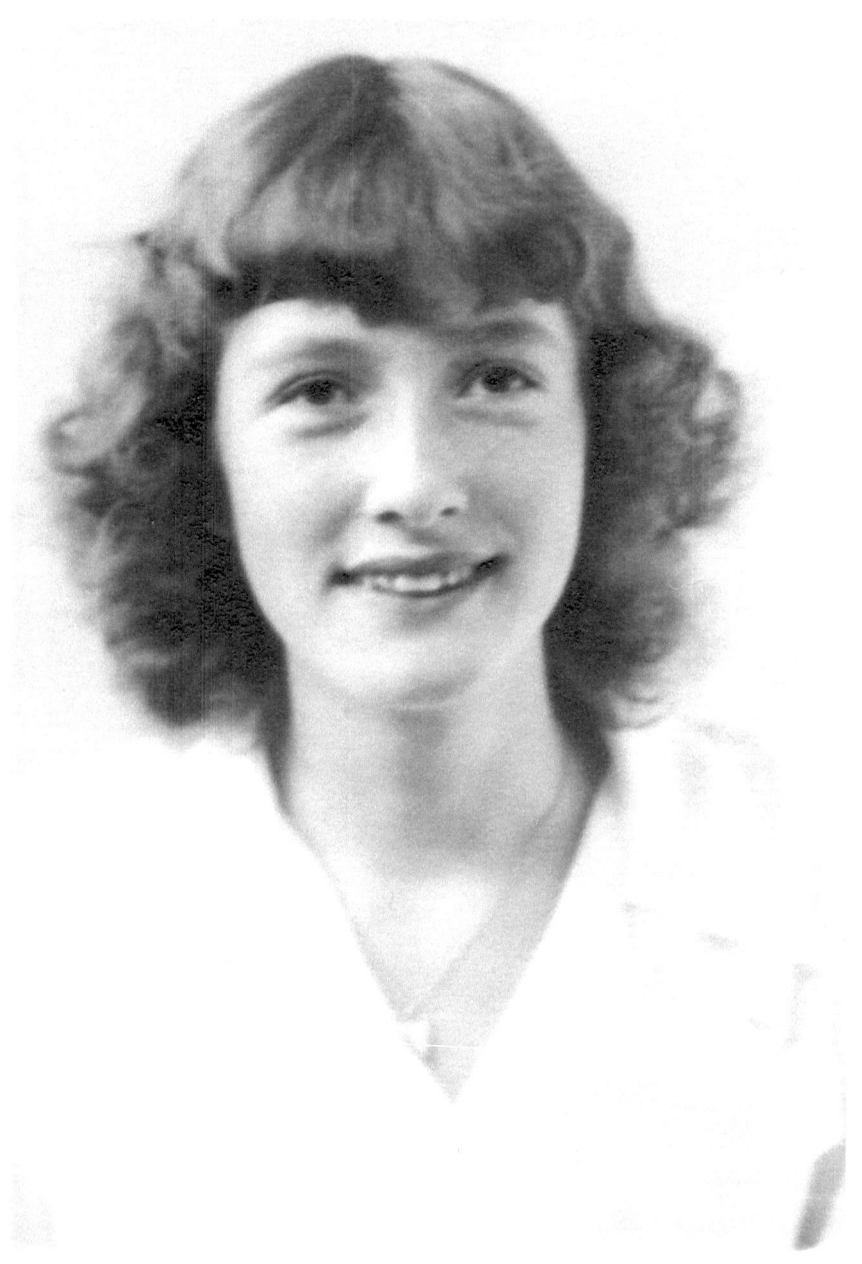

Here I am as a school girl. I was about 13 years old.

Here we are 14 happy graduating nurses from St Lukes Hospital in Davenport, Iowa. I am fourth in from the right on the back row. I was so thrilled I had become a nurse and loved every minute of it.

Here I am sixth in from the left. We wore our caps and capes with pride.

Chapter 3: My Career

Most of us had childhood dreams of what we wanted to be when we grew up. It is ironic that most of us did, or are doing, something very different from what was in our dreams. For some this might be disappointing, but for me it was a blessing. All I really knew growing up was farming. That fact that I couldn't handle horses and that tractors scared me and that I was female didn't place farming in a very prominent spot in my dreams. To tell you the truth I didn't have any strong, specific dreams of what I was going to do in the future. At that time women weren't encouraged to dream of careers. I liked to sing and suppose the idea of being a singing star like one of the Andrews Sisters must have passed through my mind. I was too practical to give singing any serious thought, though. No, I was set to coast after high school and get a job as a book keeper. That was as far as my plans went. Nursing hadn't crossed my mind until just eight weeks before I entered nursing school. That was when I was offered a full-ride scholarship to study and become a nurse. Today I have no doubt that I was inspired by God to write the essay on "Why I Want to Be a Nurse." Even as I graduated from Nursing school as a twenty-year-old girl I had no idea of the wonderful career that lay ahead of me in nursing.

Nursing had turned out to be an excellent fit for my personality I loved learning and the academic as well as the practical side of nursing was challenging and stimulating. I loved working with people which was definitely a plus for a nurse. I loved making people happy. Easing a person's pain as well as their worries had this effect on people. The fact that when I graduated I was employed by a neurosurgeon was a tremendous esteem-builder for a twenty-year-old farm girl.

Dr. Goldstein offered me the job as his assistant before I even graduated nurses training. During my last year of nurses training I had selected surgery as my focus. Surgery attracted me for three reasons: The first reason may be a little silly, but I liked going through the sterilization process and gowning up. It gave me the feeling that I was getting ready to do something very important. Of course, each surgery was very important. Second, I like the feeling of being part of a team. I wasn't the surgeon himself, but I was his assistant and played an important role in the success of each surgery. Third, there was a clear goal for each surgery. The success or failure was readily definable. I liked the intensity and the sharp focus of the work.

During my shifts I had worked with many different surgeons, Dr. Goldstein being one of them. Something about the way I assisted in surgery pleased Dr. Goldstein. He made a special request to the surgical coordinator that I always be the assistant during his surgeries. As I neared graduation Dr. Goldstein offered me a job to work for him full-time. I was flattered and immediate many surgeons had their own personal assistants. He had to pay my wages out of his own pocket. He certainly didn't overpay me for the hard work I did, but the fact that he was willing to pay what he did said much about what he thought about my skills.

Dr. Goldstein lived in Rock Island, Illinois, where he had an office. He had a second office in Davenport, Iowa. He operated at five different hospitals in the quad-city area that comprised Davenport and Bettendorf, Iowa, and Rock Island and Moline, Illinois. I had no idea how hard I was going to have to work for him when I took the job, but even if I had I would have taken the job anyway. I saw each patient before Dr. Goldstein. He didn't have to let me do this, but he wanted me to learn as much as I could. He would let me give my diagnosis before he examined the patient. I was no brain surgeon, but I got pretty good at the diagnosis after a while. He made me feel like I was part of the team and not just a hired hand.

Dr. Goldstein had five suitcases that contained all of his instruments. It was my job to carry these instruments to whatever hospital he was operating in. I carried these instruments in the trunk of my car. That was because I was on call twenty-four hours a day every day of the year. I had to let Dr. Goldstein know where I was at all times so that he could get a hold of me. During one of my bridal showers I was called to surgery and had to leave immediately. When I got to the hospital I would carry in the surgical instruments and see to their sterilization. After changing and scrubbing, I would lay out all the instruments. This wasn't as simple as it sounds and it would take up to two hours. The operations themselves could take anywhere from three to six hours. These operations were usually quite intense. Dr. Goldstein would not speak much during the surgeries. Instead, he had hand signals for which instrument he wanted. I had to watch closely so as not to misinterpret what he wanted. After working with him for a time I could often tell which instrument he was going to ask for before he asked for it, but still I had to pay close attention. As I worked with Dr. Goldstein at the five different hospitals I was pleased to gain the respect of the other doctors and surgical teams. After the surgery was over it was my job to scrub the instruments and put them away. Surgery days were often twelve hours long and very tiring. Although I only made $200 a month—or about 25 cents an hour—I found the work very satisfying

I got to know Dr. Goldstein and his wife on a personal level also. I babysat for the Goldsteins and we became good friends. He knew I was a Mormon girl and seemed to respect me for it even if he didn't know much about the Mormons. When he was in the military as a young doctor he had been stationed in Utah for a time. During that time he had boarded with a Mormon family. He told me he had been impressed with the quality of people they were and saw that quality in me also. Even so he or some of the other team in the operating room would sometimes tease me.

"We might get this operation done earlier than expected," said one.

"I bet Laurie will go out and paint the town red afterward," said another.

Dr. Goldstein would chime in here and say, "Yes, I bet she will go have a Coke!"

Sometimes Dr. Goldstein would buy me lunch. He wasn't real loose with his money and I realized he was showing me quite a courtesy in doing this. I enjoyed these non-surgical times with him. I worked for Dr. Goldstein for three years and loved every minute of it. During this time I had met Rodney Anderson and married him. Rodney's home was out West in Idaho and this is where we eventually traveled. As a new phase to my life and career began I felt a very deep sadness at leaving the employment of Dr. Goldstein. Nearly fifty-five years later he called as a frail, old man and we had a wonderful chat. He told me that I was the best surgical assistant that he had ever had. Those are words I will never forget.

My first post as a nurse in the West was in Blackfoot, Idaho. There I was just a regular floor nurse and nothing much remarkable other than my nursing career ended for a time. Rodney and I had been trying to have a baby for three years. Finally conditions suggested that I might be pregnant. I remember going to a friend in the hospital lab for a pregnancy test. I held my breath when I saw him later and he began telling me the results.

"The test says that you are pregnant," he said. "But don't get to excited because there are many false positives in these tests."

I did get excited, anyway, and later that very day when I started spotting I quit my job on the spot and went home to bed. I didn't want to lose that baby. My doctor told me that there was no use in staying in bed because if I was going to lose the baby I was going to lose the baby. I stayed in bed anyway and I didn't lose the baby. The baby was Tami and to this day I feel that my actions saved Tami's life.

It took me three years to have my first baby, but only four more years to have four more babies. Just like that Tami, Todd, Tory, Tara, and Treg made their entrance into this world. I didn't know it, but my nursing career was only on hold during these five years. Not too long after Treg's birth I was employed at the Brigham Young University Medical Clinic. Rodney was unemployed and had decided to go back to school. He was taking a night class at BYU. We were living in the basement apartment of a home that my sister, Dorothy, and her husband, Robert, were living in. Robert pulled some strings and got me a job at the clinic.

The clinic work was fun. The work was varied as BYU students came and went with medical issues that were usually uncomplicated and not very serious. I hadn't worked there long when Dr. Peterson asked me if I would come work for him in his office. He specialized in sports injuries. It was during this time that I met Johnny Miller, the very one who would become a major figure in professional golfing. He wasn't famous at the time I met him. In fact what I remember most about him was that his feet smelled very bad. When he took off his shoes I almost had to wrinkle my nose at the odor. After a year at the BYU Medical Clinic Rodney went back into Scouting and we moved to Twin Falls, Idaho. During the year we lived there I was a stay-at-home mother.

My nursing career picked back up when we moved to Burley, Idaho. I wasn't looking for a job, but as we became situated in Burley and stated getting to know people the word got out that I was an registered nurse, or an RN. Audrey Harper, the nursing coordinator at the Cassia County Regional Hospital contacted me. She told me that they were in dire need of a nurse for the LTC—the long term care unit—in the hospital. Rodney was a district executive for the Boy Scouts of America and they didn't make much money at that time. We had five children then and the idea of a little more money seemed like a good idea to me. Besides, I really liked nursing and found fulfillment doing that work. The only problem was that this position was on the night shift. I had worked the night shift as a student nurse years before and knew that I wasn't a night person. Just as when a student nurse I found that at around 2 a.m. I had to get up and walk the halls to stay awake and alert.

On one very typical night, about 3 a.m. I was scheduled to give a penicillin shot to one of the residents in the unit. The halls were silent and darkened, lit mainly by the light at the nurses' station. I don't remember being any less alert than usual as I prepared the syringe and took it into the patient's room. It wasn't until I came out and took the patient's chart to record the injection that I realized I had just given the penicillin to the wrong patient. A chill went through my heart when I realized what I had done. While most people could have had that shot of penicillin with no reaction at all, penicillin is deadly to others who are allergic. I didn't know if this patient was allergic or not, but I knew it was possible that I may have just killed him with my mistake. Standing alone in that darkened hall I certain that this was my last night as a nurse.

Just then the first part of a small miracle happened. Dr. Trehune walked through the double doors at the end of the hall into the Long Term Care unit. What he was doing on in the Long Term Care unit at 3:00 a.m I don't know, but I was glad to see him. I rushed up to him and said, "Dr. Trehune, I have just made a terrible mistake. I just gave a penicillin injection to the wrong patient."

He was well within his right to censure me for such a serious mistake, but he could clearly see how upset I was. His calm, kind response was the second part of the miracle.

"Laurie," he said. "There is nothing you can do about having given him penicillin now. There is a good chance he isn't allergic. Let's go and watch for signs of an allergic reaction." We went and observed the patient. I held my breath for fear of seeing hives appear, but they didn't. When it was clear that the patient was not allergic I felt a great relief. Color came back into my world and it seemed I might still have a career and a life yet. Dr. Trehune was calm, but seemed relieved also. He told me to record that I had given the injection and then he left. I recorded my mistake and heard nothing about it ever again. I never made that mistake again either.

Except for the night I made that mistake, night shift in the Long Term Care Unit was usually routine and mundane. Actually routine and mundane is a good thing in the LTC, because when something unusual did happen it usually wasn't pleasant. Early one morning I heard laughing and yelling coming from an older woman's room. Her voice carried easily up the otherwise silent halls. When I stepped into her room to find out what was up I found her having the time of her life. She was suffering from senility, although she didn't seem to mind. For whatever reason, she had awoken at the wee hours of the morning to paint the room with her poop. When I stepped in she was throwing the poop against the walls and up on the ceiling. The protective sidebars to her bed were up and she had smeared poop all over them as if she were finger-painting. I don't know what she thought she was doing in her head, but whatever it was there was great fun in it. What I had to do next is something they don't tell when recruiting nurses—I had to scrub the elderly resident and the room. I laugh now at the story, but while I was cleaning up I preferred to keep my mouth closed.

I loved nursing, but the night shift in the Long Term Care Unit wasn't my cup of tea. When a position opened up in the Surgical Department I jumped at it. It was ironic because the nurse whose place I took was looking for a night shift position to free up her day. My opportunity to go back into surgery was not a return to the work I did with Dr. Goldstein. I was mainly the unsterile nurse—the nurse who prepped the surgical team for surgery. I tied their gowns and was available for what ever the 'sterile' team needed. I didn't have to clean the operating room after surgery, but I was in charge of sterilizing the surgical tools. This wasn't the most exciting work, but it got me back on days and I again felt part of a surgical team as in my Dr. Goldstein days even if I wasn't quite as an important part.

I wasn't in Surgery long when Audrey Harper asked me if I wanted to work in the Emergency Room. I had never worked in an Emergency Room before, but the name itself appealed to me. "Emergency" has the connotation of excitement and importance. It seemed a place where my nursing skills could be tested in a new way every day. It would also put in contact with a wide variety of people. I didn't have to consider long at all before I accepted this new opportunity. I quickly learned that if nursing was my home, then Emergency Room nursing was the family room in my home.

The Emergency Room in the Cassia Memorial Hospital was just that, one room. It had nothing of the glamour that you see in shows like E.R. on television, but it saw it's share of life or death situations. One thing that makes E.R work interesting is the story behind each reason for the E.R. visit. Our home was only one block away and sometimes my children would come and visit me in the E.R. They would sit on one of the stools and we would talk. I enjoyed these visits. Sometimes patients would come in while they were there and my visiting child would get more education that he or she bargained for. Tory was there on one summer day when the E.R. was particularly quiet. We were chatting when a patient came in. He was an Hispanic fellow and quite drunk. His problem was clear—there was hole cut in his belly. Luckily for him it wasn't deep or bleeding too badly. He should have been in pain, but the effects of the alcohol seemed to minimize it and he was talkative. Tory sat there and listened as he described how his wife's boyfriend had held him down while his wife tried to kill him with a knife. He spoke matter-of-factly, but I wondered if Tory, who was probably 11-years-old at the time, should be hearing this. He and some of his siblings saw much more in following years on other visits.

In the medical field continuing education is very important. There are always new medical techniques to learn and new equipment to learn how to use. But even as an adult ER nurse I was still being educated on the strangeness of the world. I had been to another department in the hospital on an errand and was on my way back to the ER. There was a woman walking up the hallway. She wore a nice, form fitting dress, high heels, and a nice hat. She was a nice looking lady. We met near the entrance to the ER. I passed the woman thinking she was going somewhere else when I heard her say, "I want a sex change."

I turned and said, "Excuse me?" I had heard what she said, but I really didn't understand.

"I want a sex change," the lady repeated.

This wasn't a medical procedure I was familiar with. Sex changes were pretty much unheard of back then. I wasn't sure what to do, so I invited the woman to come into the emergency room and have a seat in one of the stations there. Then I went and found Dr. Terhune.

"I have a patient in the ER who says she wants a sex change," I said, showing my confusion.

"Oh, I know this person," the doctor said. "Let me handle it." I gladly turned it over to him.

After a while the Doctor called me into the station where I found out that the woman was actually a well-endowed man. I was shocked. Up until this moment I knew nothing of cross dressers and transvestites. My education had just been extended. A year so later a young girl 18 years of age, came running into the ER screaming, "You've got to help my brother! He's hurt!"

We hurried out to the car and carried her older brother who was in his twenties into the ER. He was doubled over in extreme pain. When we examined him we found that he had taken one of those strong rubber bands used to castrate sheep and put it around his own testicles. He had hoped to get an inexpensive, head start on a sex change operation. His testicles were horribly swollen and his pain was terrible. The doctor was able to snip the rubber band and give the boy some pain medication, but he was going to be miserable for quite a while. It looked like I was going to have to get used to those people who were unhappy with what sexual anatomy they were born with.

Over the next few years the hospital grew. A new wing was added and they built a new Emergency Department. The Emergency Department was as big and nice as I could have wanted for Cassia County. It had a nurses station, one large room that could be divided by curtains, and across a hallway there were three more smaller, private rooms. It was at this time that Fred Schloss, the new hospital administrator, changed the organizational structure of the hospital. Up until this time each section of the hospital had a lead nurse, but no more. Fred Schloss changed these sections into departments and then gave the lead nurse the title of Department Director. I was named the director of the emergency department. This was a position I loved and remember fondly.

As Director of the Emergency Department I oversaw a staff of several nurses. I was responsible for the department budget as well as seeing that the department was profitable. I liked the challenges of these responsibilities, but what I liked even more was the exciting emergencies that could come in at any minute, day or night. It wasn't as if I wanted people to get hurt and suffer pain and trauma, but when it did happen I was happy to be a part of the healing of their trauma. The adrenaline of successfully handling an emergency gave me a natural high, but there was something extremely satisfying about being the competent, capable figure a person needed in a traumatic moment. It was a position of great trust and responsibility and I held it sacred.

Not all emergency room work is exciting. There were extended times of quiet when I would take care of the paperwork involved in running the department or I would just sit and talk with the other E.R. nurses on duty. Patients would often wander in with minor injuries—sore throats, lacerations, something in their eye, and other things that, for an ER nurse were hum drum. More often than not I enjoyed talking to these people and hearing their stories. A young husband brought his wife in for stitches. I can't remember how she had cut herself, but I do remember asking the husband if he wanted to leave while the doctor stitched her up.

Showing some bravado he said, "A little blood doesn't bother me."

As the doctor stitched and I assisted I noticed that he was looking a little pale.

"You'd better put your head between your knees," I said. He did so, but a moment later I heard a body hit the floor. The young husband was out cold and we had a hard time bringing him back around. I remember the doctor was a little irritated at this.

At other times an emergency would come in that was every bit as exciting as on a TV show. I saw my share of death there and the anguish of the deceased's love ones. One afternoon the ambulance, lights flashing, brought in a heart attack victim. He was a big man who, unfortunately for me, had eaten a meal of spaghetti a little earlier and, due to the heart attack, had been vomiting. Among other things he needed immediate mouth-to-mouth resuscitation. Today an E.R. nurse would never give resuscitation mouth-to-mouth. She would use a mechanical resuscitator, but these weren't common back then. I didn't hesitate. I followed my training and gave the man mouth-to-mouth resuscitation until others could take over with the other equipment. I'm proud to say that we saved that man's life, but I have to admit that I couldn't eat spaghetti for over a year after that.

Working in an emergency room, and liking it, takes a unique personality. You have to have a kind of immunity to the pain and suffering of others. This does not mean that you must be uncaring or unfeeling. It always seemed to me that to be a good ER nurse, or just a good nurse in general, you must care about those you serve and respect their feelings; however, you cannot let your feelings hamper the quality of service you give. While I was a nurse I didn't think much about whether or not I had the right personality, but it is very clear to me now that I did. I have a son who has many children, but who has never pulled one of their loose teeth, because he can't stand the sight of their blood or the chance of inflicting pain on them during the course of helping them pull the tooth. They end up working out their loose teeth on their own. I, on the other hand, never had a problem working with the horrible wounds that would come through the doors as well as with the trauma and pain that accompanied them. Due to my training and nature it was simply clear to me that the wound needed to be tended and the pain relieved. The blood and the pain were beacons that drew me to the person in need.

I don't know what it was about Burley, but throughout the fifteen years I worked the emergency room I saw many horrible accidents. We would have doctors visiting from larger hospitals comment on the number of horrific cases that came through. I believe this was partly due to the fact that Burley is a farming community with many agricultural processing plants with machinery that shows no mercy to the human body. A woman who had beautiful, long, black hair was brought in in shock. Her hair had become entangled in a machine in a field during harvest. It had torn her scalp off with her hair. She had nothing left but her skull where here hair had been. She survived the shock of the trauma and the effects of the wound, but I know that learning to live again was difficult for her. A young man who was working on hay baler somehow got his legs caught in it. His legs weren't cut off, but chewed off almost to the hips. He didn't survive the ordeal. A middle-aged gentleman was caught in a flash fire and his entire body was burned horribly. He skin fell from his body and his body fluids, which rushed to the burns dripped onto the floor. He paced back and forth screaming and crying in pain. We couldn't touch him or get him to lie down. Eventually we were able to help him in a small way, but he died.

Not all cases were so physically horrific or physically painful. There is the psychological side to pain and death that a good nurse must be able to let go. One summer afternoon a mother pulled up into the ambulance entrance with her son and her son's leg. She had every reason to be distraught about her son losing his leg, but the salt in her emotional wound was that fact that he had lost his leg in a collision with her. They lived out in Elmo, Idaho, which was really just a geographical area that contained ranches. He was riding his motorcycle up the dirt road one direction while his mother, on some errand, was coming the other direction in her car. For some reason they collided and his leg was cut off. She had to bring him in wondering all the time if he were going to live and if he did live how to apologize for such an accident.

On another day a farmer appeared before me with no prior warning. He was carrying a young child in his arms. He startled me by throwing the child in my arms and commanded me, or it may have been "begged" me, to tell him that his child wasn't dead. But his child was dead—a death caused by injuries inflicted by the tractor tire as it backed over the him. The father had been driving. The child was feeling no pain, but I had to wonder if the father's pain I was witnessing would ever end.

On one occasion I found myself sharing a child's death with the child's mother. The child had been very ill, of what I can't remember, before her mother had brought her in. I can't remember the details, but I do remember that there was nothing we could do for the child except to make her as comfortable as possible until death came, which we knew wouldn't be long. The mother was heartbroken, yet seemed to understand that there was nothing that could be done. We brought a crib down from the pediatric ward. It seemed much more fitting than having such a small infant lay on one of the long ER gurneys. The child's mother stood on one side holding one tiny hand while I stood on the other side holding the other. I remember clearly as the child's spirit slipped away—the mother cried for her baby and I cried for the mother.

Some may think that I was unfeeling or shallow-hearted that, after having an experience such as this, I could come back to work the next day and carry on as usual. Yes, I did have the ability not to dwell on the pain and suffering I had seen, but as a fellow human being I did care. I had five young children of my own. A nightmare that I had, waking and sleeping, was that one day, when the ambulance crew burst through the doors, I would look down on the gurney to find one of my own children dying there.

I'm not one to believe that all dreams have an applicable meaning—especially nightmares. It was pure irony when, one night, my nightmare came to life. It didn't happen quite the way I imagined it. Instead of seeing one of my children being wheeled through the ER doors, my son, Todd, fell through the back door with a bullet in his abdomen. I was home at the time and it was my turn to call for an ambulance. We were only one block from my ER, but I wanted professionals moving Todd as gently as possible. I rode in the ambulance with Todd and saw my ER from the other side this time. I stood aside while the other nurses, my staff, checked Todd's vital signs and called in the doctor. How strange it was to be standing aside as a frightened mother just as I saw so many other frightened mothers do over the years. The life and death drama playing out in the ER was now very personal.

Normally when a patient leaves the emergency room that patient is no longer my concern as an ER nurse. In most cases we have taken care of the patient's medical emergency sufficiently so that they can go home and follow through with their physician later. At other times the patient is transferred from the ER to be admitted to the hospital. In either case, except for paper work, the ER has no more jurisdiction over the patient. This time, as my son was wheeled out of the ER I followed. They took him to be prepped for surgery. Again, the irony struck me. I knew and loved the surgery world. I had watched as doctors healed people through surgery. I had also seen people die during surgery. This time I sat out in the waiting area unable to take any part in my son's medical care. Here was the director of the Emergency Department, a person of influence and skill in the hospital, reduced to depending upon the skills of her co-workers. The Cassia Memorial Hospital wasn't so large that word didn't spread quickly as to whose son was having an emergency operation after being shot. It worried me that some of my co-workers might wonder what kind of mother I was to my son. That night, as Dr. Ellingham operated, I wondered myself what kind of mother I was to my son. As Todd had grown into a teenager he had grown more difficult to communicate with. Often at home he seemed unhappy with his parents and family. Much of this seemed to be due to just growing up, but as I waited for word about whether he would live or die I wondered how much I lacked as a mother in raising him.

After three hours of exploratory surgery focused on finding the damage the .22 caliber bullet had done as it zigzagged through his abdomen, Dr. Ellingham finally emerged to tell me that, "Your family home meetings must really pay off. The bullet missed everything important in his abdomen." What Dr. Ellingham meant by "your family home meeting" was my family's religious faith. He was not a Mormon, but he knew I was. He also knew that we had Family Home Evening every Monday night without exception, something our Church encouraged us to do to make a stronger family. This news, given so confidently by Dr. Ellingham, made the sun rise even though it was the middle of the night. It took time, but Todd went on to fully recover and my nightmare was cheated out of its horrific ending.

I had been in charge of the Emergency Department fifteen years and things were running smoothly. Staff morale was good. We were profitable. Our reputation was good. I got along well with the doctors and others on the hospital staff. I didn't think things could get any better. One day Dr. Ellingham came to me and asked me if we could have a chat in private.

"Laurie, I've been watching you and how you run the Emergency Department and I am very impressed. You have excellent medical skills as well as organizational and management skills." He went on to say, "I've thought about this carefully and I would like to sponsor you to become a Physicians Assistant."

I was caught totally off guard. A physician's assistant was one step away from being a doctor. They could treat patients, prescribe medicine, and run their own practice. Just as I had never dreamed of becoming a nurse before I got that scholarship I had never dreamed of becoming a physician's assistant. And just like nursing school here the opportunity was opening up before me. I was extremely honored and flattered by Dr. Ellinghams's offer. Now that he offered this opportunity I wanted almost more than anything to take it. When the scholarship was offered for nursing school back in 1950 I had asked my Mom if I should take it. "Of Course!" had been her reply. Oh, how I wished the decision could be so easily made this time.

I thought about this opportunity for a couple of days. It would require a year of schooling that I would have to take in Pocatello. It was a long way. I could drive there every day, but I would have to leave early and come home very late. On my own I could manage this. But I had five children to take care of. They had a father, but his work took him away from home for long periods of time. Going to school to become a physician's assistant would be right next to abandoning them. I knew if I told them how much this would mean to me that they would want me to go. However, I also knew that they didn't understand how hard this would be on them and the family. After considering it for a couple of days it was clear to me that to accept this opportunity would be to sacrifice my family.

I remembered how badly I had wanted children and how difficult it was for me to get them. I had been willing to give up nursing to have them and I was willing to give up being a physician's assistant to keep them. It was very difficult for me, but I declined the offer and explained to Dr. Ellingham why. I don't think he fully understood how I could turn down such an offer. He didn't understand the importance of family in my life and the risk I would run in taking this training. We remained on good terms, although I had to watch as he offered the opportunity to someone else and she went on to make good with it. My heart ached a bit to let go of this opportunity and watch someone else take it, but it was endurable because I had made a careful decision and I know I did the right thing. To this day I wonder how different my life would have been if I had taken that opportunity. It would have been wonderful to be a physician's assistant and work as a doctor. I would have risen that much higher up in my career and would have been very proud. I'm certain, though, that the price for that pride would have been very dear. I don't know how good of a mother I was to my children, but I do know that I was good enough that to have abandoned them at that time in their young lives would have had a negative life-long effect that could not have been defended in any other achievement.

Perhaps as a reward for my decision, or maybe it was in consolation, I had the opportunity to become an emergency medical technician—an EMT or Paramedic. I often saw the ambulance crew when they brought patients to the ER and I became friends with them. It was suggested that I take EMT training.

"Even if you don't want or have time to ride with the ambulance the training will only make you a better emergency room nurse," he said.

The training was given right in the hospital and it seemed like a good opportunity. I like learning and gaining new skills and jumped right in. With my training and experience it wasn't difficult although I did learn a lot. I earned my EMT certificate and later my advanced certificate. I did get to ride with the crew on several occasions. It was like being in an on-site ER. Most of the runs I went on were not very exciting, maybe a broken bone or a banged head, but nothing much more. There was one accident that was memorable. A small plane had crashed with a pilot and a passenger. The plane had come straight down and might have well just exploded when it hit the ground. No one survived. The ambulance was there to pick up the pieces—literally. I had seen a lot in the emergency room, but I'd never had to walk around looking for what was left of human bodies after an explosion. I have a strong stomach, but even today that memory sends a shiver up my spine.

It was years later that something else completely unexpected happened. I found myself staring up from a gurney at the faces of my staff in my own emergency room. I had no feeling and could not move any part of my body below my neck. Less than an hour before an ambulance crew, not my own, had very carefully extracted me from my car. I had been traveling with two friends to see Shoshone Falls when a farm truck had unexpectedly turned left in front of us on a country road somewhere near Hagerman, Idaho. The friend who was driving swerved to avoid a collision and the car rolled three times and flipped end over end twice. Both friends walked away from the accident. I wasn't so lucky. It does seem a miracle that I wasn't ejected from the car and killed as it tumbled which is what usually happens. When the car came to rest my head was pressed between the two parts of the front seat and the rest of me was up on the dashboard. I remember telling the paramedics that I couldn't feel anything.

In all my days in the emergency room I had never dreamed of being brought in myself in such serious condition. The nurses and doctor on duty were given word that an automobile accident victim was being brought in and the condition of that victim, but as usual no names were given. They were as surprised to be looking down at me as I was to be looking up at them. Just the day before I had been in full command of my body, my life, and my career. I had built the very emergency department I now lay in almost from the ground up. Now, suddenly, on what started out as a fine day to go see Shoshone Falls, I found myself lying in my own ER, unable to move, with what appeared to be a broken neck.

Other than the broken neck my condition was stable and I was whisked out of the ER to radiology for x-rays. The x-rays were inconclusive on if my spinal cord was severed. The doctors, who I knew so well, made the decision to send me to a hospital in Pocatello, Idaho, that specialized in spinal cord injuries. I wasn't aware of it as they wheeled me out through the ambulance doors that my career as an ER nurse was over. If I had been aware of this fact perhaps I would have thought that my life was over also.

During the first two weeks at the rehabilitation center I lay a complete quadriplegic. I had learned that my spinal cord hadn't been severed, but was only bruised. This diagnosis was good and bad. It's always good to learn that your spinal cord isn't severed. On the other hand, with a bruised spinal cord, there is no telling how much of a recovery can be made or how long that recovery might take. In spite of the unknown future I remained upbeat. The nurses said they liked coming to visit me because I cheered them up. The truth was that they knew something I didn't and were just waiting. Finally, it happened. One day my predicament became fully clear to me. I couldn't move below the neck. I was completely helpless. I had seen others in the same predicament and didn't want to learn to live as they lived. I broke down and cried my heart out. What was I going to do? This is what the nurses had been waiting for. Just as I recognized reactions caused by the trauma of the emergency room, these wonderful rehabilitation nurses understood the course of emotions of someone suffering a severe spinal cord injury such as mine. They came and consoled me until, with a final sob, I got control of myself.

"Now the real healing can begin," one said.

It was soon after I had had my emotional breakdown that Dr. Wood and Dr. Ellingham drove to Pocatello to visit me. It good to see these two men who I had worked so closely with in the Burley ER. Although their main reason for coming was just to see me and chat, they also took the opportunity to unofficially examine me. I learned later that after they left they both agreed that I would probably never walk or use my arms again. Dr. Wood thought I would lie helpless in a bed the rest of my life. I'm glad they didn't tell me this. I might not have been willing to believe that I had just felt a prick of the pin for the first time. I might not have noticed the movement in my finger. My spinal cord was healing. With these small encouragements I began physical therapy. At first we just concentrated on feet and fingers. Eventually it was legs and arms. Even as my muscles started responding I didn't have full control over them. I quickly learned to live one day at a time. Six weeks after I had entered the rehabilitation center I was well enough to go home. I wasn't the same spry woman I had been that fine morning six weeks before, but I walked into my house with leg braces and crutches and a slow gait. My hands and arms were weak, but I could get them to do what I wanted. My mind and will were strong—even stronger than before the accident. I stayed home for a few weeks and then decided that it was time to get back to work. Sitting around the house was not something I was used to. I was the department head of the Emergency Department. I had been away too long and there was much I needed to do.

The next morning I walked into the ER ready for work. That made for quite an entrance for a person who had lain there two months before with a possible severed spinal cord. My staff was happy to see me. I didn't recognize it at the time, but they were also surprised to see me. You see, I wasn't scheduled to come back to work, but no one had told me this. The administration at the hospital were aware of the progress I had made in rehabilitation, but they were also aware that I was a woman that needed leg braces to walk and had no strength in my hands and arms. In my mind I had proudly walked back through the ER doors. They didn't see me walk as much as hobble back through those doors. None of my nurses said anything about their surprise. It was Dr. Wood who took me aside and, although happy to see me back, expressed his concern.

"What would happen if someone came in here and fainted and hit their head on the floor because you didn't have the strength to catch them?" he asked. "There could be a lawsuit."

I agreed that he had reason for concern there, but I was getting stronger. I was determined that I could do the job.

Dr. Wood really got my attention when he said, "It's very possible that you could lose your nursing license if there are any questions about you working with less than full strength."

This scared me a little, but I went back to work the next day anyway. I couldn't see any other life than running that emergency department. Until someone physically stopped me, that was what I was going to do. It didn't take the hospital long to get control of the situation. Two days after Dr. Wood had spoken to me I received a call from Fred Schloss, the hospital administrator. He wanted to see me in his office. I should have known what was coming, but I was still hanging on stubbornly to the idea that the accident hadn't changed anything.

Fred Schloss was a good administrator and a decent human being. This was actually born out by what happened in his office that day. But at the time what he did hurt me deeply. Audrey Harper was sitting in his office when I came in. If being called in to the hospital administrator's office is bad enough the "bad" is multiplied by 10 when the nursing supervisor is there also. I took my seat and we immediately started with small talk and pleasantries about my recovery. They were both very happy to see me on my feet again. To say they were surprised to see me so soon back at work was an understatement. At this point the conversation turned to the heart of the reason they called me in. They were aware that I was back at work in the ER. They were also aware that I was only able to walk with braces and that my arms were weak. I had to agree with them that we didn't know when I would get my strength back or if ever would.

"Laurie," Fred said. "For the sake of the hospital and your sake we have to remove you from your position as director of the Emergency Department effective immediately."

Those words sent an icy sword between my ribs and through my heart. For a moment there was complete silence in the room as I tried to comprehend the words I had just heard. I had just lost my position. They were taking the position I loved just a little less than my children away from me. I had been in an accident, but I would get better. The braces and the weakness wasn't my fault. I would get better. I needed just a little more time. All these things whirled through my head, but still I said nothing. And then the tears came. I covered my face with my hands as I sobbed openly. I hadn't cried when my son was brought in for emergency surgery. I hadn't cried when I was brought in with a possible broken neck. But losing this position felt like the keystone of my life's arch had just been pulled and now my life would collapse. Audrey, who I knew was there to sanction Fred's actions, momentarily dropped the mantle of Nursing Supervisor and cried with me in sympathy.

Mr Schloss sat uncomfortably for the minutes it took for me to get a hold of myself, but when I did he indicated that he had more to say.

"Laurie, you are too valuable of an employee to lose. Your current condition may not allow you to work in the ER anymore, but there is a new position opening up that you would be perfect for."

With red eyes and a burning in my throat I listened as he told me how the hospital needed a full-time quality assurance person to deal with all the new regulations the government was creating to oversee Medicare patients. This position could only be filled by a nurse who not only knew the current medical procedures, but who also had a rapport with the doctors since these new regulations would have a great effect upon how they treated their hospitalized patients. The writing was on the wall and it was written clearly. I could no longer be department head of the emergency department. My stubbornness had been beaten down and I could see that they were right—I physically didn't have the strength to continue. This new position appeared as a piece of gravel next to the diamond of the ER, but I needed employment both for the money it brought and because I needed to be needed. I accepted the new position, but when I walked out of the hospital that day I walked out with a broken heart.

No matter what happens life has a way of moving on; it is just a matter of keeping up. I had seen people lose loved ones in the ER. From the anguish I witnessed at those times I am sure that some of them didn't feel like living another day. In months following the loss of my position, sometimes I would see one of these people at the store or at a city event. They would be talking with someone and even smiling. Life had learned to deal with their loss and move on in life. Unlike them I had only lost a position, not a loved one. Life could certainly go on for me. In fact for a person who should have been killed in the car accident, or at least been confined to a wheel chair, I had every reason to move on with life. And I did. I am a survivor.

The new job was definitely a change of pace. There was no trauma or drama, no need to know where the medical equipment was kept for life-or-death situations, and there was no adrenaline. However, my job was very important for the profitability of the hospital and was taken very seriously by the administration, the doctors, and me. I spent all my time studying patient's paperwork and on the phone talking to the government regulators. Although the work was boring I did a good job. Every once-in-a-while my new job would take me to the emergency department. I hated going there anymore. It was like running into an old boyfriend who you had never quite gotten over. I would leave feeling depressed, but I dealt with it. On March 27th, 1994, after ten years of quality assurance work well done, I retired. Friends and acquaintances gathered for a little retirement party. We ate some refreshments, exchanged handshakes and hugs, and then I walked out of the door for the last time. I was beginning a new life at that time and I never looked back.

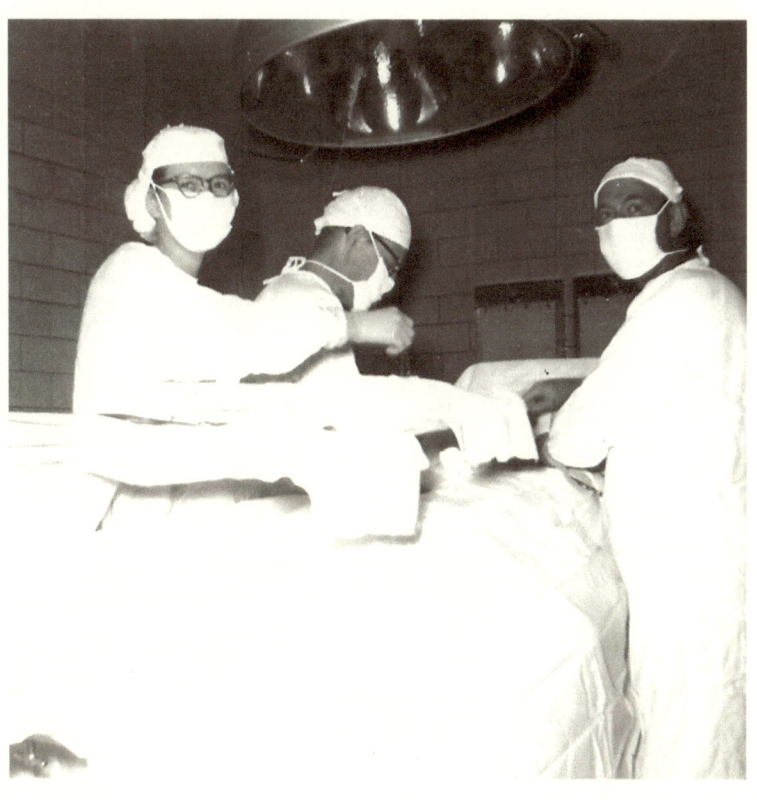

I am scrubbed in on this actual surgery with Dr Agnew, and Dr Brown and we were doing a cholecystectomy. I loved this work. Taken 1953.

This is Dr Stanton Goldstein, the neurosurgeon who took me under his wing and turned me into his assistant in surgery and at his offices. What an opportunity for an Iowa farm girl. Taken in 1953.

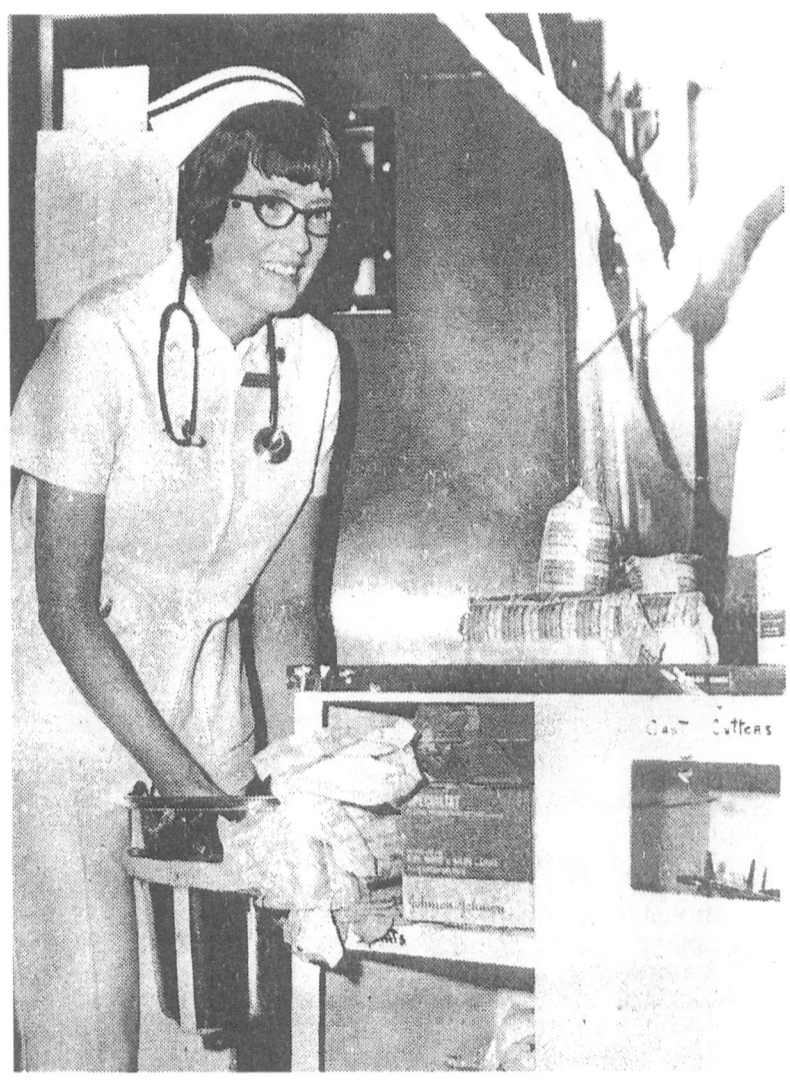

Now I am the supervisor of the Emergency Room in Cassia Memorial Hospital in Burley, Idaho. I worked here for fifteen years and loved the work.

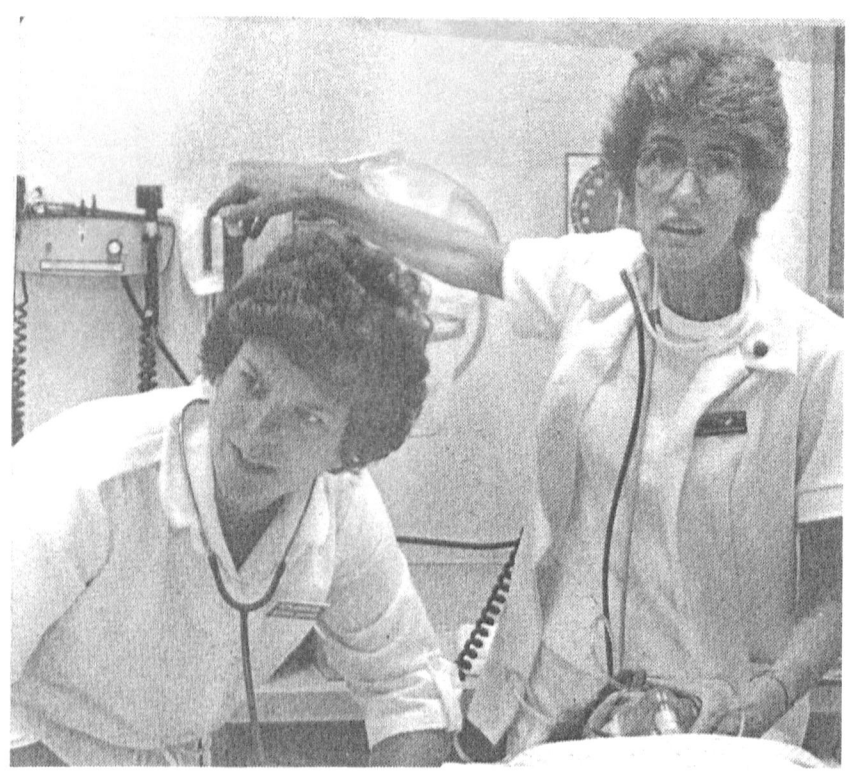

We had a disaster (an incident that involves many patients coming in at a time) and my co worker and I are doing a triage and keeping track of all the patients.

Chapter 4—Family Life

Growing up in the '40's and '50's marriage and family were always a hoped-for possibility for the future. No, I didn't long for or pine for a husband, but unlike today where marriage seems like a secondary goal for many women, marriage back then was still desired by most women. After my Grandmother Dickinson introduced me to her neighbor as "her ugly, string-bean of a granddaughter" I never saw myself as attractive or desirable by boys. In high school when I saw a boy and a girl holding hands I sometimes felt a pang of jealousy and wished that could happen to me. My junior year in high school I did have a boy friend, but we broke up at the beginning of my senior year. That was about as far as romance took me before college. Even if I did have the typical school-girl daydreams about boys and romance the lack of romance never got in my way of participating in activities and having a good time with friends.

While in nurse's college my major focus was on the schooling itself. There were books to study, tests to prepare for, and work shifts to complete. My hard word paid off and I graduated second in my class. Even with my hard work I had time to date a little. While student-nursing in the psychiatric hospital I met a student minister who was working there on a three month internship. We began dating and enjoyed each others company. I remember he gave me a cross necklace as a gift one evening. After his three months were up he went back to Ohio and we fell out of touch.

I can't remember how I met Rawley. We dated for a time and he even introduced me to some of his family. Rawley was a school teacher. I remember his first letter to me and how shocked I was at his bad spelling. I wondered how he could be a school teacher while being such a bad speller. This was such a turn-off to me that I rather abruptly broke off seeing him. I was always worried that I would come down from the dorms and find him waiting to talk with me in the reception area. That never happened. These starts and stops in dating didn't bother me. I wasn't looking for romantic relationships. I was thoroughly engrossed in my medical training and didn't need much else in my life.

Romance found me anyway. Towards the end of my college training my sister Dorothy and I decided to go home for a visit. It was a forty mile trip by bus. It was in the Greyhound bus terminal in Davenport, Iowa, that I met a young soldier named Rodney Anderson. He was was a soldier in the U.S. Army and was on a three-day pass. His sister had married and moved to Iowa. He was on his way to visit her. He looked very handsome in his uniform. He boarded the same bus I did and it wasn't long before we were in conversation. Dorothy thought is was unladylike of me to speak so freely with a stranger, but I was naturally outgoing and could talk with anybody. Rodney found out I was a nursing student and told me that his sister was studying nursing also. She was having difficulties in her studies and he wondered if I would write to her and encourage her. I agreed and we exchanged addresses.

Our next communication was by letter. It is ironic that I, an up-and-coming nursing student who valued education and proper English, attracted men who could not spell. In Rodney's letter I saw spelling that was so bad that the letter was hard to read. I had already dropped one young man who was interested in me because of his bad spelling. So why didn't I drop Rodney? I don't know. He lived so far away and couldn't get a three-day pass very often. I could have easily written to him and told him not to bother. But I didn't. Maybe I didn't because Rodney was handsome. Maybe I didn't because in spite of his horrible spelling his letters were warm and colorful. I think one of the most likely reasons I didn't write Rodney off was because Rodney was bringing me something more precious than life itself—it was through Rodney that I found the Church of Jesus Christ of Latter-Day Saints. I believe that God had a hand in our meeting and influenced me to accept Rodney in spite of his spelling. Rodney had come home from a mission just days before being drafted into the army. The gospel was very important to him and it didn't take him long to bring up the Church of Jesus Christ of Latter-day Saints even though I made it clear that I was born and bred a Methodist. The role he played in my conversion to the Church developed an initial bond between us.

Rodney courted me via three-day-passes. Even though Davenport was outside the geographical range allowed for a three-day-pass from Camp Riley, where he was stationed, he would come up anyway. When in town he would stay with the Drakes, some local members of the Church.

One night Rodney and I had planned to go to a movie. Instead of a movie Rodney surprised me by taking me to a local LDS member's home where the stake missionaries began teaching me about the restored gospel. One of these stake missionaries was Robert Drake. Later he would teach, baptize, and marry my sister Dorothy.

At the time I didn't feel a need for anything more than the Methodist's version of the Gospel in my life, but I was willing to listen. The conversation was lively and fun—I saw to that. I was no push-over. I asked lots of questions and made them use the Bible to support their position. On the other hand, even if I did spar with the missionaries and Rodney, inside me the truth of what they were teaching me was all-too-apparent. When finally asked if I wanted to be baptized into the Church of Jesus Christ of Latter-day Saints the only truthful answer I could give was, "Yes, I do." Originally it was Rodney who was supposed to baptize me, but when he arrived for the occasion on his three-day-pass I was sick and we had to postpone the baptism. Rather than wait for the next three-day-pass Robert Drake baptized me in a chapel in Rock Island, Illinois, in May of 1953.

During the time I was being taught the Gospel I was still in school, but I had moved out of the dorms and was living with a family in Davenport, Iowa. The father of the family had been a patient at one of the hospitals I had worked at as a student nurse and we had become acquainted. He had taken a liking to me and invited me to take a room in his home where he lived with his wife and two young sons. This family was devout Methodist and I attended Church with them every Sunday. They became my family away from home and I learned to love them. I went on family outings with them, babysat the boys, and got along very well with them.

On the day of my baptism I came home with wet hair.

"Have you been swimming?" Mrs. Sawyer asked, doubtfully. She had never known me to swim before.

"No," I said. I was feeling warm and happy about my baptismal experience, but I hadn't really thought about how the Sawyer's might react. Joining the Church of Jesus Christ of Latter-Day Saints was as natural to me as growing up. It didn't occur to me that others might not see it that way.

"Then why is your hair all wet?" she asked.

"I've just been baptized," I said.

"What do you mean 'baptized'?" Mrs. Sawyer asked. "Weren't you baptized into the Methodist Church when you were a baby?"

I began to feel a little worry in spite of my happiness. "Yes," I said, "but the Methodist's couldn't answer all my questions. The Church of Jesus Christ of Latter-Day Saints has answered all my questions. Today I was baptized into that church."

Mrs. Sawyer, who was usually quite a cheerful person, looked puzzled and displeased. "The Church of . . . what?" she asked.

"The Mormons," I said, using their more commonly known nickname.

Her puzzled looked turned to outright shock. "You joined the Mormons?"

I nodded. Some of the warmth I had been feeling was ebbing away.

There was silence in the living room for longer than I liked broken only by the ticking of the clock on the shelf. "So you won't be going to church with us anymore?"

"No, I guess I won't," I said.

"And Mormons don't drink coffee, do they? So you won't be drinking coffee with me and Henry anymore?"

"No, I guess I won't," I said. I hadn't thought about these things before now.

There was another silence, but shorter this time.

"I don't know that you belong here anymore," she said. Her voice was cold and near tears. "In fact maybe you better leave right now."

I looked at Mrs. Sawyer a moment wanting to say something, to explain why I had done what I had done, but a wall had suddenly gone up between us. Thomas and Martin, her two young sons had walked into the room during this exchange drawn by the feeling of crisis. I had held their hands while taking walks with them and played many games with them, but they were looking at me now as if I were dangerous. Not finding any words I turned, went up to my room, and threw all my things into my suitcase. When I came back downstairs Thomas and Martin stood across the room each holding sheet of paper up like some kind of protest sign. Scribbled several times down each sheet were the words, "No Good! No Good! No Good!" The words had the desired affect and hurt me deeply, but I knew the boys were innocent. They were only writing what their mother told them to. Without saying anything I went out the front door. I don't know that I recognized it at the time, but as the door closed behind me I stepped into a better, brighter world in spite of the momentary disappointment.

"Did you question your decision to be baptized when you found yourself outside their house with your bags?" my son asked, when interviewing me for this book.

"I didn't," I said, without even thinking about it. "I wasn't happy about being expelled from their home and lives, but I no more questioned being baptized into the Church than I questioned the need for taking my next breath. I had done what I had to do and their response to my action, although hurtful at the time, was nothing more than a disappointment that healed quickly as my life went on."

While it is true that my marriage to Rodney ultimately didn't work out, I will be forever grateful for the pearl of great price that he brought me in the form of the restored Gospel of Jesus Christ. The Gospel became the foundation on which the rest of my life was built. To it I owe all of my peace and joy.

Rodney had proposed to me during the Christmas season of 1953. We decided to wait to be married one year after my baptism so we could be married in the temple. During this time I finished my schooling and went to work as a surgical assistant for Dr. Goldstein. Rodney was honorably discharged from the Army and got a job in Rock Island, Illinois, as a pole lineman for the Iowa-Illinois Power Company. He lived with the Drakes, the parents of Robert Drake—the stake missionary who baptized me. When the year was up we married first in the LDS chapel in Rock Island. This would make travel arrangements easier for our trip to Utah to the temple. It would also allow my parents and my friends, who weren't members of the Church, to participate in our marriage. The very next day after our civil marriage we started our journey to the Logan Temple in Logan, Utah, where we were sealed. After visiting with Rodney's family we returned to Rock Island, Illinois where my married life began.

About a year later Rod and I moved to Idaho where Rod would begin his career as a district executive in the Boy Scout's of America. We rented a basement apartment in Blackfoot, Idaho. I went to work as a floor nurse at the Blackfoot hospital. In addition to adjusting to marriage the focus in my life at this time was on starting a family. I wanted to have children. It seemed to me that marriage wasn't marriage without children. After three years we still didn't have any children and I was frustrated. Rodney and I had tests done, but they were inconclusive as to why I was having trouble becoming pregnant.

"Will I ever have children?" I asked the doctor.

He looked thoughtful and said, "Let me put you on my adoption list. Having children may be difficult for you." I already knew that, but he wouldn't commit more than that to the possibility of me becoming pregnant.

I wasn't ready to settle for the adoption option. Rodney and I did the only other thing that we knew how to do at the time—we went to the temple and asked a member of the presidency for a special blessing. I don't remember the blessing being particularly noteworthy with grand promises and the appearances of angels. It was a quiet, normal kind of blessing where they confirmed God's love for me and the righteousness of my desires. Then they promised me that I would become pregnant in due time. That was comforting and gave me faith and hope, but at the same time it was one of those promises that could take years to be realized. I left the temple that day at peace, but resigned that I might remain childless for some time. Wasn't I surprised when the "Lord's due time" came much sooner than I expected. It was just a few weeks after that blessing when I realized that I might be pregnant. I used my connections at the hospital to get a pregnancy test right away.

"Am I pregnant?" I asked the lab technician as soon I walked into the lab.

His answer was indirect, but gave away the test result immediately. "Don't get your hopes up, Lori. These tests are often wrong."

When I started spotting later that day I promptly quit my job and went home to bed.

My doctor told me, "There's not need to stay in bed. Either you are going to have the baby or not." That was a fatalistic attitude that you don't see much in doctors today. I stayed in bed anyway. The time didn't go too slowly. I kept busy with various projects. The ward gave me a calling in the Relief Society. I was to call the sisters to remind them of upcoming events and to check up on them. Carol, from the upstairs apartment, would come down almost every day to check on me. She was a young mother who already had five children—all girls. She would feel my growing tummy and say, "Yes, there's something in there. It's getting bigger!" Her companionship added a sparkle and a joy to my first pregnancy. Carol became a very good life long friend.

At nine months I went in to the hospital to have the baby. If getting pregnant was difficult having the baby was more difficult. Today doctors order caesarian sections at the drop of a hat. Caesarian sections were rarely done back then. That procedure would have been in order for my first delivery. After I had been in labor for some time I knew things weren't going well when I heard the doctor say, "Put her under." They gave me ether and I don't remember anything after that. I understood that they had to use forceps during the delivery. It wasn't too long after regaining consciousness that I became acutely aware that I had torn very badly during the delivery. It was months before I could sit comfortably. It didn't matter because I was now the mother of a little girl. We named her Tami. There is something about a first baby that all the acquaintances enjoy. For some time, at church, I would only get to see Tami as she went by from one person's arms to another. Everyone wanted their turn to hold her.

By today's standards I would be seen as impatient and perhaps a little strange. Tami was only nine months old when I was already wanting another baby. I asked my doctor if there was any way that would make getting pregnant again easier. I was still remembering how difficult it was to get pregnant with Tami. I don't know what the doctor said or did, but I'm pretty sure I went home pregnant. It was just nine months later that I had Todd. There were just eighteen months between Todd and Tami. Todd must have primed the pump because with only eighteen months between each after him I had Tory, Tara, and finally Treg. In just seven years after I asked for that special blessing I had five children. Be very careful what you ask for.

Raising one child is an adventure. Raising five . . . well, raising five children is five adventures. My life was kept full of the typical things that accompany motherhood: diapers, chicken pox, bed wetting, school programs, band performances, plays, first dates, first loves, anger, fear, hugs, graduations, marriages, and grandchildren. Although these things are "typical" in general, to each particular mother these events are the color and the soundtrack to the movie of her life. If I were to write a book on each of my children you might just be able to catch a hint of the vivid color he or she added to my life or the melodies and chords I hear when their names are mentioned. Instead, I can only offer glimpses of some of the intersections where their lives are intertwined with mine.

Tami—emotional, expressive, beautiful, talented. Tami was so limber that she could sit on her head. With only minimal lessons she became adept in gymnastics and tumbling. She often entertained her family and friends with tumbling routines across the front lawn. She started her own business and taught tumbling to many girls and boys in the garage-turned-studio. Gymnastics wan't the only thing she was adept at. One summer she came home from Boy Scout camp signing in American Sign Language. A deaf troop had spent a week at that Scout camp and she learned quickly. The bud of this new talent may have died on the vine, but when she returned home she found a new family next door with a deaf girl her age. A friendship developed and Tami quickly progressed beyond the alphabet to fluency in the language. I've watched as she has gone on to a successful career as a professional interpreter for the deaf. I watched in joy as she married and bore three sons. I hurt with her as she divorced and lost custody of those sons. It was then that I saw what Tami was really made of as she swam against the current to show her love for her sons while she put together a career, found a new love, and started a new family. She is a good daughter.

Todd: handsome, mysterious, accident prone, adventurous, kind. Todd fell from a ladder while picking cherries breaking both wrists.

Todd was hit by a car while bicycling near his elementary school and received 164 stitches in his neck and head. Todd was shot in the stomach with a .22 caliber rifle. Todd broke his ankle playing softball. Todd sawed off the end of his finger while working on a carpentry project. Todd was bit by a rattle snake while building a trail with his father. I could go on, but it would become boring. Todd has never been boring to me. Between wondering what is going to happen to him next and all the girls he has introduced me to he keeps me on my toes. He is the only one of my children who never went to college (until recently). Instead he joined the Army, learned three languages, traveled the world, and served in three wars: both Persian Gulf wars and Afghanistan. His divorce saddened me greatly, but his extreme dedication as a father to his children, to his parents and to his brothers and sisters makes me proud to be his mother. He is now very happily married and will graduate in another year from college. He is good son.

Tory—peacemaking, studious, talented, devoted. Tory was one who always wanted to do what was right. During one family night when Rodney and I were getting after the kids for some bad behavior Tory spoke up and said, "So what can I do to make things better?" That pretty much sums up his nature. I don't remember this but he tells me that once he found a *Playboy* magazine in the ditch across the street. In all earnestness he brought it into the house to show me what a horrible thing he had found. He was about 12-years-old at the time. He promised he hadn't looked past the cover. I took the magazine and, shaking my head and "tut tutting" in disapproval thumbed through the entire magazine before throwing it away and telling Tory I was proud of him. Tory surprised us all when he tried out for a part in the choir for the school musical "Lil' Abner" and got the lead part. Tory was the first to graduate from college. He earned a master's degree in English. In spite of my joy in being a grandmother Tory made me wonder if he was ever going to stop having children. He has at eight. His dedication to his family, shown by the amount of time he spends with his children, is an inspiration. He, too, is a good son.

Tara: tall, pretty, confident, level headed, companionable. Tara and I have had our personality differences that have caused us to eye each other warily. It says a lot about her ability to love and forgive that we are great friends today and spend a lot of time together. Except for the time she burned the skin off her feet when she spilled boiling water on them, she grew up with few crises. She showed a flair for adventure when she spent two summers living almost homeless with her father in remote parts of Alaska. She showed her independence when she went on a successful mission to South Carolina in spite of the interest of young men around her. She was very level-headed and knew what she wanted in life. This showed while several young men courted her. Most of these young men were aspiring college students and one already a college graduate. The latter took her for a ride to look at homes-for-sale. He offered her any of these homes if she married him. She turned him and all the others down for a fellow who seemed to have lower aspirations, but who had gained her heart. She probably has the most successful marriage of all my children. What makes me most proud was how, with two children, Tara made the decision to go back to school and get a four-year degree in elementary education. Her commitment and perseverance in life make me proud. She is a good daughter.

Treg: easy going, dead-pan funny, smart, dependable, my baby. You know Treg is the baby when you hear him say from the living room where he is lying on the floor watching TV, "Milk, Mom!" and I get it for him. Treg was the icing on the cake of my children. Although I was older when I had him than any of my other children, he never gave me any gray hairs. He played the trombone and graduated in the top ten in his high school class. He grew up happy, went to college, got married, had four beautiful children and continues steady in employment that he loves. I find great comfort in his steadiness. He is a good son.

Today most women have a difficult time imagining what it would be like to raise five children and hold down a full-time, professional career. They might think that it would be difficult and too much sacrifice. I remember very little sacrifice that seemed like sacrifice. Instead I remember wonderful times that I would never had experienced without my children. Below is an essay I wrote after a memorable summer with my family.

Fantastic Summer of 1970
By Laurel Anderson

This is an account of our summer in 1970 while Rod was employed by the Snake River Area Council Boy Scouts of America.

June 5, 1970, we packed and left for Safulu Mala Tasi at Banbury Hot Springs located near Buhl, Idaho. We spent two weeks there at the Guide Patrol Camp. It rained the first three days and was so cold that we rented a cabin that had a kitchen, bedroom with two double beds, and a bathroom. Tami, Tara, Treg, and I slept there. Rod and the two older boys slept outside in our tent. We swam three or four times a day in the warm water of the hot springs. It cost us $78 for two weeks. We ate all our meals at the campsite and Rod cooked for us and his staff of eleven boys. After it warmed up and dried out the camp was great fun.

On June 20 we left Safulu Mala Tasi and headed for Camp Bradley, which was about a four hour drive away and twenty-three miles north of Stanley, Idaho. It took us 7 1/2 hours to get there as somehow we got off on the wrong road. We discovered we were on the wrong road when we saw a sign telling us that the pass was closed due to snow. We turned around and eventually found the right road. We pulled into Camp Bradley about 3:30 PM.

John Hill, Camp Director, put us in cabin #5, the furthest from the center of camp, but the largest. It had an upstairs which consisted of one large room under the eaves. The main floor was one large room too, with a front and back door. The three oldest children slept upstairs and the rest down. The big fireplace kept us warm. Todd and Tory became very good at starting fires. Rod kept a good supply of firewood for us to use. There was a big old-fashioned cook stove that smoked so badly we only lit it once. There was a sink that ran cold water only, and there were four big windows (one of which Tami broke while playing "handy-over-the-cabin." All-in-all it wasn't a bad place to call home.

The first few nights the kids upstairs seemed to dream a lot. We'd hear them walking around and talking in their sleep. One night one of the boys got up in his sleep and must have thought he was in the bathroom as he urinated on the floor. The floor had big cracks in it which happened to be right over the head of his sleeping parents below. The dripping soon hit their faces, jarring them awake very rudely. By the time their mother hollered and their dad got upstairs to check, all were sound asleep. We don't know which one it was as no one admitted being up in the night.

The ground squirrels were plentiful. Quite a bunch had their home under our cabin. We sat on rocks beside their holes and put food out for them to eat. They'd poke their heads out and if we sat very still they would venture out and eat. We spent many hours watching them. They finally got used to us and they'd eat right by our feet. One day we had a surprise as their babies came out. It was fun to watch them grow during the summer. We tried to trap them and did manage to catch a few, but they always got away. They were so quick. We never hurt them and we wouldn't have kept them anyway. They even came into our cabin through a hole by the fireplace.

We caught a darling baby rabbit one day on our way to the lake. We had him three days before Tory left the door to his cage open and he got away. He was so cute—he ran all over the cabin and on the bed. He crawled down into Treg's coat sleeve and went to sleep once. We later found him dead out by the cabin; we were all very sad. Some of the Staff caught another one later, but we let him go. There were chipmunks all over, too. They would eat out of our hands. One ran up Tami's leg.

The deer were plentiful in camp. They'd come close around our cabin. They didn't seem to be afraid of us. It was interesting to watch them and we were all eager to see a buck with a rack on his head. They liked to eat in the early morning and evening by the hot springs that were just below our cabin.

It was a mile to the lake. You could get there by trail or road. We usually took the road as it was easier walking. The three oldest kids took a swim check and passed. They had to swim 100 yards in the cold lake water. Todd only made it 50 yards in the first time, but with his Dad's help he tried again and made it. The boys took out canoes and rowboats and became very good at handling them—Todd took his mom for several rides.

In the camp was a natural, warm-springs pool. The kids swam practically every day. Treg and Tara learned to swim this summer. Tara learned the crawl stroke and backstroke. She wouldn't dive, though. Treg learned to tread water and swim on his back. He tried the crawl stroke but he wasn't coordinated enough to rhythm breathe. He also learned to dive and it was very funny watching him. He had very good form; he was just like a fish in water.

One day when Troop 13 was in camp (from our ward in Burley) they grabbed me and threw me in the pool—clothes and all. It was fun and I didn't mind.

Tami went to Legrand, Oregon, to visit Bob and Dort. She was gone about three weeks. She took the bus from Twin Falls, coming back to camp July 31st. She was in Legrand for her 12th birthday.

Tara got a black eye while at camp. She and Pam Gleed were playing the autoharp and the edge of it struck Tara by her left eye.

Rod, Todd and Tory went on an overnight hike July 30th. They carried packs on their backs. It was so cold at night that Tory and Todd slept in the same sleeping bag and there was lots of frost on them the next morning. They caught sixteen fish and had a real good time.

The next evening Rod and I took a drive with Dr. and Mrs. Paul Heuston in his 4-wheel drive. We drove to Sea Foam Ranger station and then up a real steep road to the top and walked to the lake that Rod and the boys had fished at the day before. It was beautiful! It was truly God's country.

Camp was at 7000 feet and the lake must have been 1000 feet higher. The lake was thick with jumping fish.

The kids and I took several hikes—out to Marsh Creek, up on Twin Peaks behind camp, and to the lake. The forest was thick with pines and wild flowers and the air was cool and clear.

I was camp nurse and was kept busy with the sick and hurt scouts. They seemed to like me and I enjoyed mothering them. We only sent three scouts to Sun Valley for treatment. Pretty good record! We had a diabetic once that was in a semi-coma but got him back on his feet.

There were campfires each Monday and Friday night. We only missed one, I think. The kids learned the songs and had fun with the scouts. Treg was always riding on someone's shoulders.

Rod was in charge of the white water trips down the Middle Fork of the Salmon River. He made four trips. They'd put in at Dagger Falls and float 106 miles and drop 4000 feet. They had nine rafts and about 45 people on each trip. He was in camp the first two weeks, then out two, in one and then out two. The weeks he was in camp he made a Ferris wheel as a pioneering project with one of the troops. It really worked and the kids rode it. Even I had a ride.

During Rod's third trip down he fell out of the raft at Water wheel Rapids and floated 200 yards where he was finally able to get out. Wearing a life jacket he floated down feet first. The water was so low that many rocks stuck out of the surface. He'd hit the rocks with his feet and it would whirl him around to hit another rock with some other part of his body. He narrowly escaped from hitting the cliff at the end. He said it was a wild ride. He also lost his glasses.

We got an education in sign language for the deaf. There was a partially deaf boy on the staff who taught us. There was a deaf troop from Gooding, Idaho that was in camp two weeks. We could communicate with them quite well. Tory, Todd and Tami became quite adept at using the signs.

We made two or three trips to Stanley, but other than that we were in camp all summer—nine and a half weeks. I did not have to do any cooking all that time as there were two cooks who cooked for the entire camp. The boys on staff did the dishes. I washed three times a week and hung the clothes up to dry. They had an automatic washer the first few weeks but it broke down and I ended up using an old conventional washer that wouldn't even drain. I ironed our bath towels on the kitchen table.

We packed and left for home on August 20, leaving behind beautiful, cool, mountain living and many fond memories of our summer of 1970.

The kids grew up, graduated from high school, and left home one after the other. For many couples this is a time when husband and wife get to spend more time with each other. Instead of caring for children 24/7 they get to enjoy grandkids on the weekends. With their free time they can travel or pursue other common interests. This wasn't going to be with Rodney and I. As the children grew up Rod and I were growing farther apart. It wasn't long after Treg left home for school and mission that I filed for divorce from Rodney. I think this caught almost everyone by surprise. There were very few outward signs of the unhappiness I felt in my marriage that anyone would have noticed. There was no infidelity on either part and no scandalous arguments. There was only a lack of emotional connection between Rod and I. Rodney was taken by surprise by my desire for a divorce. That he could be surprised at my unhappiness was a major part of the problem. We could not communicate in any meaningful way and it seemed clear to me that we never would. Rod, unable to understand my unhappiness, was against the divorce; however, I was determined. After twenty-eight years of marriage, and after successfully raising five children, my marriage to Rodney ended.

Divorce is a life-changing event for any normal human-being, but divorce was just one of the dramatic changes taking place in my life at this time. My career as an RN and director of the Emergency Department was just coming to an unexpected end due to my accident. All of my children, who had been the center of my life for the past 26 years, were now living independently. Add my divorce to this and it was as if my life up to this point was just a dream and I was now awaking to something I didn't recognize. Everything I knew was coming to an end. What I didn't know was that something new was about to begin.

Motherhood took over first place from being a nurse. I loved being a mother and here are my first four children taken in Brigham City, Ut, Tami 4, Todd 3, Tory 2 (not wanting his picture taken) and Tara just a baby.

I started a tradition on Christmas Eve with a special Christmas meal. We had the best dishes and glassware, and the meal always started with Pumpkin soup. Some of the T's still hold this tradition in their families today. All five T's are in this picture with Treg in the highchair. This is the Christmas of 1966.

These are my five T's today. Tami, the oldest on the right, with Tara, # 4 on my left. In the back stands my three sons: Todd, #2, Tory #3 and Treg my baby #5.

Here is what makes families perfect—a large group of happy wonderful grandchildren.

My Grandma Dickinson, my Dad's mother, and my five T's on a visit to the farm in Iowa. Tami, on the left, with Treg, Tara, Todd and Tory.

Chapter 5—Beginning Again

During my years as an emergency room nurse at Cassia Memorial Hospital, while I was still raising my children, I worked closely with many other hospital employees. Most of these employees became friends of mine at one level or another and are fond memories to me now. One of these employees was the department head of housekeeping. Her name was Elsie Jensen. She was a very professional woman who took her job seriously. At the same time she was the mother of six children. In these two ways we shared many things in common. During the years we were acquainted at the hospital we had no idea how much more we would eventually share in common.

My son Tory was employed by Elsie for two or three years when he got a job in housekeeping at the hospital. Tory and his big brother, Todd, were employed by Elsie's husband, Reed, to thin and hoe beets on his farm just across the river from Burley. Todd and Tory worked shoulder to shoulder with Elsie's children out in the beet fields during the hot summer days. They took sides as the Jenson sons and daughters started clod fights in the arguments that picked up and died away as the girls passed the boys as they worked their way up and down the rows hoeing out the weeds. It was no secret that Todd found Eileen, one of Elsie's daughters, attractive. The fact that this attraction went nowhere in the end has saved us all some complex explanations today. This will be made clear shortly.

As Elsie struggled with her cancer I struggled with the end of my marriage and the difficulties I knew it would raise for my children. Then came the car accident that very nearly took my life and ended my career as an emergency room nurse. Elsie passed away during the time I was struggling to regain the use of my body. I worked so hard to learn to walk again only to find they wouldn't allow me to continue as the director of the emergency room or as a nurse in any capacity—yes I could walk, but I didn't have the strength I needed as a nurse. The job in quality assurance they offered me looked dreary in comparison, but I took it anyway. I was on my own now and needed a way to support myself.

I was sitting in the hospital cafeteria eating lunch. Nothing about my life was the same as it had been just a year before. My marriage of 29 years had ended two years earlier. My children were gone. A career that I loved had ended unexpectedly. My body was weak and barely under my control. I had plenty of reasons to feel sorry for myself. Maybe somewhere amid all of this I did feel sorry for myself, but the feeling didn't find fertile soil inside me. I don't know that I had any happy dreams for the future, but I knew that I still had a life to live and I was determined to live it even if it were emptier than it had ever been before. Little did I know that the beginning of a very rich future walked through that cafeteria door that very day in the form of Reed Jensen.

There were many people in the cafeteria at that time and I took no notice of Reed until he approached my table and asked if he could join me. Reed was Elsie Jensen's husband. Before her death I had known Elsie quite well on a professional level, but Reed was just barely an acquaintance. He was a successful farmer and his work rarely brought him to the hospital. I may have seen him at various hospital social functions where he accompanied Elsie, but I took no notice of him. On this afternoon, however, as he stood at my table asking if he could join me, our situations had changed. He was a widower and I a divorcee. We had both become single again in unpleasant ways, but our lives were continuing in spite of that fact.

When I divorced Rodney I had made no plans for the future as far as personal relationships went. After twenty-nine years of marriage, raising five children, and having 52 birthdays it never occurred to me that there might be another meaningful relationship in my life. When I allowed Reed to sit down and we started chatting it didn't take long before I sensed that something was drastically different about this casual conversation. Reed was not saying anything alarming or even anything that would have caught the attention of someone eavesdropping at the next table—it was just that he was speaking to me as a single man and I was responding as a single woman. The absence of the fence of marriage, even when neither of us was hunting for a mate, opened possibilities that made the expected topics of conversation we engaged in more electric for both of us. I remember feeling strangely refreshed and happy at the end of our conversation that afternoon when I went back to work. I would not have admitted to anyone, not even myself, that I was interested in Reed as being anything more than a warm and pleasant human being. At that point that is all he was, albeit one who had unexpectedly and quite easily swept away the rather blue mood I was in. No, there was no love at first sight for me. It wasn't until he called and asked me out the next evening that I realized that it might be possible to love again.

On our first date we watched a movie at my house. Reed had found out that one of my favorite movies was *Singing in the Rain* and he brought the video from the video store that he ran on the side. We hit it off and started going out often after that. Reed was still uncomfortable being seen dating in his hometown, so we would often go to Twin Falls to eat or to see movies. The forty mile drive to and from Twin Falls gave us an opportunity to talk leisurely with each other and really get to know each other. I loved how Reed would talk and talk. He listened well, too. It was clear to me that we would never tire of each other.

Eventually our relationship grew more serious. For the second time in my life I had the experience of being taken to meet a boyfriend's parents. Actually, they were Elsie's parents to whom Reed was very close. It was only my love for Reed that got me to the door of their home.

How do you approach the parents of the deceased woman you might replace? Surely they would see me as an interloper; as someone who would destroy all their daughter had built. After all those years with their daughter and after fathering their grandchildren surely they could not accept me coming into the picture.

His mother-in-law, Jenny, and his father-in-law, Rulon, were out back in the garden when we got there. When we got to the back door Reed asked me to wait there. He may have been a bit nervous to introduce me to his in-laws, but now that I know Reed better I know he just wanted to surprise Jenny and Rulon.

"I have someone I want you to meet," Reed said. Jenny immediately ascertained that it was a woman Reed was speaking about. There was no uneasy silence. There were no furtive glances my direction.

"Oh, my!" Jenny said touching her gardening dress and then her hair. "Why didn't you tell me you were bringing company and I could have been more prepared."

Jenny greeted me with all the warmth and happiness that a girl could hope for. All my anxiety was swept away in a moment. Rulon grew a beautiful rose garden. He was known to give a rose to a visitor whom he liked. Before Reed and I left that evening, Rulon had handed me a rose. That rose has long ago faded, but the joy and warmth of that meeting is still fresh and in bloom.

Reed and I made marriage plans. It was clear to us that this was the right thing to do. It wasn't so clear to our children. With his six children and my five there were a lot of feelings and opinions on the matter. Although Reed and I didn't ask for our children's permission we did our best to be respectful and let them speak their concerns. We held a big family meeting where all the children were present. I imagine this would have been extremely awkward had the children been strangers to each other. As it was the children knew each other fairly well. In fact my son Todd would certainly have dated one of his soon-to-be step sisters had he not already been going steady with someone else. Although there were loyalty issues with having their parents remarry, the children had no grudges or reason to distrust each other. At the end of the meeting some of Reed's children still weren't happy with our decision to marry so quickly after the death of their mother, but there was no hostility. I even remember that some of our kids ended with reminiscing about old times out in the beet fields and about other encounters with each other.

On August 23 of 1986 Reed and I were married in the Jordan River Temple in Utah. It was a beautiful day in my life. I married Reed feeling that he was my soul-mate and this has borne out through the years since. Many of our children were at the wedding. Some were reserved in their feelings about the event, but all were cordial. Others showed complete acceptance of our marriage. Lloyd, one of Reed's sons, was particularly affirming in his acceptance of me in his life. He came up to me after the marriage ceremony and told me that while in the temple he had a confirmation from the Lord that my marriage to Reed was blessed by the Lord.

"You will be a grandmother to my children," he said.

These words meant so much to a young bride (at least I felt 21 again that day) who was marrying into a family in which the children were already grown. There were other of Reed's children, like Lloyd, who accepted me quickly and gave me their loving embrace. There were a few who wondered about my motives in marrying Reed and saw me as trying to replace Elsie, who had birthed and raised them. Over the years their feelings have changed and they now accept me for what I am—a companion for their father who has sought to enrich Reed's life, not in place of Elsie, but in addition to Elsie. Now, even one who had the most difficulty in accepting me will call me up on Mother's Day to wish me a happy Mother's Day. I am grateful for this. I am "Grandma" to Reed's grandchildren and that brings me great joy. It gives great credit to Reed's children, though, that Elsie is not forgotten by their children, most of whom never met Elsie. Every-once-in-a-while one will tell me, "I know that you are not my real grandma," but then they will hug me and call me "Grandma."

My own children had their own struggles, not so much with my second marriage, but with the divorce. They all loved Rodney, their father, very much. This wasn't charity on their part. Rodney was a very good father who earned their love with all the time he spent with them. None of the positions he held over the years required him to be separated from the children much. On the contrary, he was able to include the children in his work and he did. They spent summers with him at the scout camps he either ran or had part in. They spent summers building trails with him in remote, but beautiful, mountain locations. Todd was his assistant as river guide on the Salmon River. Tory would come home from school for lunch and Rodney would take him to his Kiwanis Club luncheons. Todd, Treg, and Tara spent a summer with him during his two years in Alaska. So they were close to their father and perhaps felt a little betrayed when I divorced him.

Just as a couple of Reed's children had difficulty in accepting me marry their father, a couple of my children had more difficulty in accepting my divorce. Tory was one in particular. He never vocalized anger or tried to cause any discord in my life, but it was clear by his infrequent contact with me that he was very hurt. I would see his children once or twice a year which wasn't nearly enough and was much less than was possible. It wasn't until his first son was twenty-years-old and going through the temple in preparation for his two years of church service that this hurt was suddenly and quite unexpectedly healed. Reed and I had driven down to the Manti Temple to attend this special temple experience with Tory, his wife, Barbara, and their first son, Tory. It was during this temple session, where the Spirit of God is felt so strongly, that Tory's hurt was healed and we shared a joyful embrace. Although all of my children struggled in their feelings, they treated Reed and I well enough from the beginning and have accepted our marriage fully now. Reed has not replaced a grandpa for my grandchildren, but is just another grandpa to love.

I jumped into life with Reed with both feet. Reed was a farmer and after I got off work for the day I would go out to the fields and find Reed. I would sit in the tractor with Reed as we made our way slowly back and forth across his fields in Southern Idaho preparing the ground for sugar beets, potatoes, or wheat. I rode in the big harvest trucks with him as they were loaded with grain or sugar beets or whatever else he was harvesting. We would talk and talk trying to catch up on a lifetime. When break time came we would pull out a cooler that held our lunch and eat in the truck.

I had moved into the home that Reed had built for Elsie. It was a beautiful home far out in the country, but it being "Elsie's" home I made sure not to change anything. There was a portrait of Elsie on the wall above the fireplace mantle. One day Jenny, Elsie's mother, came over to visit. When she saw the portrait of her daughter she said, "What is that doing there?" I thought it was obvious what it was doing there and had trouble finding words to answer. Jenny wasn't really wanting an answer. Before I could say anything she went over and took it down. "This is your house now," she said. Jenny took the portrait home with her. I know Jenny loved and missed her daughter very much, but Jenny had a strong sense of the present and of moving forward. I learned much from this.

Despite Jenny's help I moved forward slowly in making a home of my own. I respected Elsie's memory and tried to be considerate of the feelings of her children. Some of them noticed right away when Elsie's picture disappeared. After a time we moved to a second home on farm property west of Burley. This was a nice home also, but it being farm property it still wasn't one I could make my own. After living there a couple of years Reed was able to buy me a home of my own on the Declo Highway above the river. We lived there many years in that first home that was truly Reed and Laurie's. Both sides of the families came to visit often—sometimes separately and sometimes together. They got along well together. It didn't take long—in fact I didn't even notice—when both sides of the family were just "our" family to Reed and me.

Reed and I hadn't been married too long when we had family move in with us. Reed's mother, Lola Jensen, had been diagnosed with Alzheimer's Disease. As it progressed she needed constant care. Reed and I took turns with his two sisters and had Lola stay with us every third month. Taking care of an aging parent in one's home is not a task to be taken lightly, but taking care of a parent with Alzheimer's is a task of the same magnitude as raising a child again. The difference is that the Alzheimer victim has already lived his or her life and gained your love and respect. It is they who are forgetting everything about their life and reverting back to childlike behaviors. Lola lived with us for a couple of years. Reed was a very loving son and did his best to make her feel comfortable. At times though she would become stubborn on some subject or behavior and Reed would argue with her as if she were the child and he the parent.

Lola could be unknowingly very entertaining to us. One day we came home from an outing and as she walked past her bedroom she stopped and with complete surprise in her voice said, "This looks just like MY room!" There were times when Reed and I wanted to go out together without her. We had to be a little tricky at these times because if she caught wind that we were going out she would assume she was coming with us and run and "dress" for the outing. She would return with layers of pants and skirts and blouses on. Then there would be tears as we tried to make her understand that she was to remain behind with another family member while Reed and I were going out.

As Lola's Alzheimer's progressed she forgot who I was although she still remembered Reed. She often would ask Reed who I was. He would respond, "She's Laurel. She's my wife, Mother!" She would stare at me with wondering eyes, but accept it. One night she kept us up. While reliving some past part of her life she kept going into the kitchen to cook. Reed or I would get up and take her back to bed. On one of these cooking excursions we awoke to smoke. She had caught a towel on fire at the stove. After this we didn't sleep well the rest of the night. The next afternoon, while I was napping, Lola, who somehow knew I was there, would work her way off the couch where Reed had set her and come to my room.

"Who is that?" she asked when Reed intercepted her.

"You know who that is, Mother," he said. "That is my wife! Now leave her alone so she can get some rest. You kept us up last night." He then led her back to the couch.

It wasn't long before she slowly worked her way off the couch and again came to my room and called out to Reed asking, "who is that?" Reed would explain again and take her back to the couch. On her third attempt to get off the couch to come investigate me Reed was there to set her right back down. This made her angry. She sprang off the couch this time as if she were twenty-years-old.

"You son-of-a-bitch," she said. "I want to know who that woman is!"

This was especially amusing because Lola was the sweetest woman and had never used a bad word in her life.

I had gotten to know Lola before her Alzheimer's had set in and found she was very easy to love. As everyday tasks became more and more difficult for her to do I stepped in. I showered with her, curled her hair and dressed her. Although she had lived a full life and felt no regrets or pain as her Alzheimer's progressed I felt sad as she eventually forgot who I was and then who Reed was. It still was a very sad day when she died.

Sharing Reed's mother with him in the manner that I did was a wonderful opportunity to become a part of Reed's life in a way that was not possible in any other way. Ironically the same opportunity came knocking for Reed.

My father, Lloyd Dickinson, had lived a very independent life. He operated a successful Iowa farm until he retired. When my mother, Grace, succumbed to Alzheimer's he didn't put her in a home, but took care of her himself until her death in 1984. After that he moved into an independent living home until he was 97 years old. It was then he decided he wanted to be nearer his children. He had three daughters to choose from and I was honored that he chose me.

Unlike Reed's mother Lloyd had his full mental faculties to the day he died. He was very old and needed daily help, but his mind was sharp and his memories were clear. Lloyd and Reed had much in common, both being farmers, and enjoyed each other's company immensely. Dad was an old-school farmer from the days of horse drawn implements. He farmed relatively few acres compared to Reed and raised everything from pigs and chickens to corn and milk cows. Reed, on the other hand, farmed thousands of acres with a fleet of trucks, tractors, and combines and tended to farm only one crop at a time. However, Reed had ventured into raising beavers on the side and had his own animal experiences. In spite of their farming differences, or maybe because of them, Lloyd and Reed spent hour after hour, usually during dinner, telling farming stories and laughing at each other's experiences.

In addition to just talk Reed helped Lloyd with some health issues. Lloyd's feet had poor circulation which threatened to become a very serious problem. In the evenings Reed would sit on the floor and wash, massage, and dress Lloyd's feet. Reed and Lloyd became great friends. Dad lived with us for about two years before he died in February 1995. He made one last journey back to Iowa where he was buried next to Grace in the Masonic Cemetery in Tipton. I don't think it is often that people who are married a second time later in life get the opportunity to get to know a mate's parents in such a personal manner as I did Reed's mother and he did my father.

Second marriages on their own account are wrought with challenges. But when they also involve eleven children and such close association with in-laws the challenges can be insurmountable. These elements were indeed challenges for Reed and I, but challenges have a way of turning into blessings if met with strength, love, and faith. Reed and I were able to give each other strength, we shared love, and together we exercised faith. Now my life is filled with loving children (eleven), beautiful grandchildren (forty-five), and the sweetness of great-grandchildren (thirty one).

In 1984 my life had every appearance of being over: my body was weak, my career as an emergency room nurse was unexpectedly ended, my marriage was finished, and my children were grown and gone. If someone had told me that there was another life in store for me rich in love and companionship and family I would have told them they were crazy. There is a philosophy with many adherents that any happiness a person has in life is an accident and that pain is the natural product of this world. I have felt my share of pain and unhappiness, but the joy and happiness I have and am experiencing has far outweighed the bad. Happiness is not an accident, but is a gift from God and available to all who look for it and have hearts open to receive it.

This is a unique picture—we three were awarded employee of the year in our departments and this picture has me, on the left, with Reed's first wife Elsie, in the middle. Later I would take Elsie's place as Reed's wife after her death. She and I were good friends.
Taken 1977.

Reed and I are taking a walk in Washington DC during our mission there in 2005. This was an exciting time in our lives.

Reed and I are in San Diego at a grandson's wedding in 2011. At this time in our lives it is thrilling to see our grandchildren marry and begin their journey like we did some years back.

Chapter 6: Retirement (or Not)

In 1994 my friends and associates threw me a little party and I walked out of the hospital retired after twenty-five years of employment there. I had been employed as a registered nurse for 41 years. That is quite a career for someone who at age 17 didn't want to be a nurse. In 1995 Reed turned over all farming operations to his sons and effectively retired. Now what to do? Reed and I had been employed full-time all of our lives. Never before had we had to give much thought to what to do between the hours of 8:00 am and 5:00 pm. I suppose I could have taken up painting and Reed golf, but neither of us had any inclination to do so. Our first inclination, with so many children between us, was to spend more time hosting and visiting them. There were (and still are) a steady stream of baby blessings, baptisms, graduations, and missionary farewells. It takes one well-organized grandma to keep track of 65+ birthdays. But even all these family matters don't take up all the time. Reed and I had plenty of energy and talent left and needed a place to apply it. What is more, we needed a place where we could apply it together.

While living in the house by the Snake River, Reed and I had started serving in the Logan Temple of the Church of Jesus Christ of Latter-day Saints. We would travel to Logan twice a week early in the morning and return home late the same night. It was only natural for us to be drawn to temple work because temple work is all about family. I was also drawn to temple work because the entire nature of the work is service. There is no pay for the work and very little recognition. So what is the draw? Health! I find myself getting up in the morning with a purpose for the day. I stay relevant by exercising my talents in a place that needs them. I find meaningful associations with others who also find joy in serving. At the writing of this book I am pushing 80 years old and still find myself useful and needed, not just by my family, but by the world. What makes it even better is that Reed and I are able to perform this service side-by-side and continue to enrich our marriage. Perhaps most importantly of all is that by being in the service of our fellow man we are in the service of our God. I find great peace while in service to God.

Serving in the Logan temple was part-time service. Reed and I discussed our situation and decided we were ready for a full-time mission. We were getting ready to retire and thought it was time. About five years before this we had friends who were serving in the Temple Square mission of the Church of Jesus Christ of Latter-day Saints. Through conversations with them we made it known that we would be interested in serving a mission at some point in the future. I don't know how knowledge of this conversation remained in existence for five years, but Reed and I got a call from the Temple Square mission asking if we were interested. We were very interested and would have gone right away except that our situation had suddenly changed. My father, Lloyd Dickinson, had come to live with Reed and me. When I explained our situation to the caller, he said, "That's all right, then. Your father is your mission right now. We will check back at a later date."

Today, when I think of this, I take joy in the support I felt from the Church when it came to taking care of family. As described in the previous chapter my father was with us for two wonderful years before he passed away. Serving him and enjoying his presence was a life-sweetening experience. When my father died we took him back to Iowa to be buried next to my mother. Two weeks later the Temple Square Mission, with which we had had no contact with for over two years, called to find out if our status had changed and if we could come serve. It didn't take much thought before we realized that yes, we had nothing to keep us from moving on to this next step in our life.

Temple Square

"Having nothing to keep us from serving a mission," is arguable among grandparents. While it is true that we were retired and no longer had an elderly parent who depended on our care, what about our children and grandchildren? While serving part-time in the Logan Temple two days a week we still had five days to do with as we wished. On a full-time mission we would be committing all

91

of our time to the goals of the particular mission where we would be serving. Due to our commitment we would not be able to leave the mission to attend the blessings, baptisms, and graduations that would most certainly come along. Because the commitment level is so high making the decision to serve a full-time mission for the Church is very serious. One part of me told me that to go on a mission would be to neglect my grandchildren. But the other side of me told me that I could not sit around waiting for things to happen in my grand-children's lives when I still had so much to give the world. My service on a mission would enrich my life which in turn would enrich my grand children's lives. There would still be letters and phone calls and even visits. Our family life would continue and be even more colorful from our service experience. Reed and I made the decision to serve a full-time mission for the Church.

In May of 1995 Reed and I officially received our call to serve in the Salt Lake Visitor's Center in the Temple Square Mission located in Salt Lake City, Utah. This was such an exciting time in my life. My three sons and one of my daughters served full-time missions for the Church. My other daughter had served a stake mission. Now it was my turn.

Although the Church of Jesus Christ of Latter-Day Saints is a worldwide church with branches and wards in hundreds of countries, Temple Square would be considered by most members everywhere the center of the Church. It is the heart of the place where the Saints gathered from around the world in the early days of the Church when its very existence was threatened by persecution and prejudice. Not only does it host the Salt Lake City Temple and Mormon Tabernacle, both of which have architectural and historical significance, Temple Square has an extensive visitor's center that can accommodate thousands of visitors at once. It is a favorite place for members of the Church to visit if they happen to be traveling through Salt Lake City. It is also a major cultural and historical tourist attraction. Tens of thousands of tourists visit Temple Square every year. It was in this bustling, beautiful place I would be serving for two years.

Reed and I moved out of our home on the river and into a small apartment near Temple Square in Salt Lake City, Utah, where we could walk to work if we chose. Compared to my beautiful home on the river the apartment was cramped and we had neighbors through thin walls. But the work soon enveloped me and the cramped living arrangements didn't matter anymore. Some of my children thought that going on a mission to such a desirable place as Temple Square was not a real mission. It is true that couples are called to places where living can be much more difficult such as in Central America or India. In these missions the couples must learn new languages, struggle to understand a different culture, and deal with being so far away from children and grandchildren. None of these things were factors in my first mission. We were only four hours from home. Many of our children lived just a short drive away. Reed and I were able to attend many of our favorite basketball team's games—the Utah Jazz. But the Lord's work is the Lord's work wherever it may occur and I put in the steadiest and longest hours of my life those two years on Temple Square.

There were 180 sister missionaries and 37 couple missionaries in that mission. Missionaries were on duty from 9AM until 9 PM when Temple Square closed for the night. The sister missionaries mainly worked directly with the visitors answering questions, giving tours of the tabernacle and assembly hall, and taking groups, small and large, through the visitors center where they can learn much more about the doctrines and teachings of the Church of Jesus Christ of Latter-day saints. These sister missionaries come from all over the world and thus among them speak many languages. One of my favorite sights during this mission was to see these sisters lined up outside the tabernacle each pair holding a different nations flag in front of them. When the visitors, who, also, came from all over the world, came out from listening to the practice or performance of "Music and the Spoken Word" on Sunday mornings they would spot their nation's flag and know that they could go speak to someone who spoke their language. These young sisters were required to memorize lengthy narrations that went along with the many different tours.

The missionary couples were normally assigned to information desks and other posts that didn't require language and memorization skills. Even though it wasn't required, Reed and I decided we wanted to do more on this mission than sit behind a desk and give directions. We decided that we would memorize the narrations also which would then give us the right to work out among the visitors like the young sisters. On the one hand I was in my sixties and long out of school so the memorization (and there was a lot of it) seemed a little daunting. On the other hand, being an emergency room nurse and an advanced emergency medical technician had required me to keep studying through the years so I knew I could do it. And Reed? His mind was sharp and the memorization posed no real difficulty for him. I am so happy that Reed and I decided to memorize the narrations. Doing so expanded our mission experience exponentially. We did work out among the visitors and had the joy of momentarily being a part of families of all color from places around the world. For the most part was delightful getting to know them for that few minutes to an hour we were together.

There were those few, though, who were troubled and some others who were just plain rude. In one instance I was approached by couple who appeared to have questions. But the man's question was one that most people would not be ungraceful enough to ask. He wanted to know about the "secret underwear" we wore. I actually kept my composure and explained as best I could, although a little more chilly than usual, and they went on their way. The memory of being asked about my underwear by a stranger in a public place is amusing today although it makes me wonder about some people.

On another occasion I was approached by a man who wanted to know if I believed in Christ. Well, Temple Square being built and owned by the Church of Jesus Christ of Latter-day Saints I thought the answer was obvious. When I told him I had a strong testimony of Jesus Christ I was taken aback by his telling me that no, I didn't. It turned out that because I didn't believe in Christ the same way he believed that I didn't believe in Christ at all. I politely, but firmly expressed my difference in opinion and again bore testimony of Jesus Christ. He seemed to grow bored with me at this point and excused himself.

In a third experience I was working in the main visitor's center when I was approached by a woman. Her husband trailed behind and her kids were running about exploring. She wanted to know where she could have a look at the golden plates from which the *Book of Mormon* had been translated. She had been told about these either on a tour or before coming to Temple Square. When I explained that the angel that led Joseph Smith to them had taken them back she exclaimed rather loudly, "I knew it! I knew they didn't really exist." I remember her husband being a little embarrassed by her demonstration and leading her away.

I tell these three experiences I guess because they are different from the thousands of more pleasant encounters I had with visitors. Reed and I had to be on our toes when working with the visitors but with a little effort and with God's grace we were able to develop a genuine love for them as fellow human beings.

Reed and I adapted so well to the work on Temple Square that we were eventually made training coordinators. This turned out to be quite a responsibility. Every week we were to hold a training class for all 227 missionaries in the mission. To make this more manageable and keep the work going we split the missionaries into two groups so one group could serve the visitors while the other was in training. Each week we had to prepare talks and training activities. We had to keep coming up with fresh ideas that would make the training effective and keep the missionaries attention. We would give various missionaries training preparation assignments and we would bring in guest speakers. One guest speaker was Michael Balam. He has had a very distinguished career as a singer. We just happened to run into him as he visited Temple Square and had a nice chat. Since a training class was about to begin we got rather bold and asked him if he would like to come say a few words to the missionaries. He very gracefully accepted. It was a very memorable training class.

Reed and I had committed to an 18 month mission. When we neared the original ending date President Witt called us in and asked us if we would be willing to extend our mission for another six months. If we agreed it would mean six more months in a small apartment instead of my beautiful home on the river. It would mean six more months of separation from family. It would mean six more months of hard work seven days a week. The truth is, when we were asked to extend, none of these things actually passed through my mind. Very simply the work was fulfilling. Each day was exciting. The feeling of being needed and of making a difference is very gratifying. Sitting in a bigger, nicer home on the river couldn't touch it. As far as family went, we were in touch with them weekly through phone calls and letters. Our work in the mission added a vitality to our communications and to our relationships that is unique in life.

In addition to extending our mission I was asked to be the administrative assistant to President Witt. Being offered this position was an honor because it held so much responsibility, but it also made me anxious because I learned that President Witt considered the administrative assistant I was replacing perfect at her job. My responsibilities included keeping track of all the missionaries who were just arriving as well as those departing. I would meet with each sister missionary and couple on their first day in the mission, brief them on how it all worked, and give them their first hug. I was involved in keeping track of and communicating their assignments during the duration of their mission. Every week President Witt would write personal letters to a certain number of the missionaries and I had to make sure the letters were mailed. There were many more duties similar to these and Reed and I continued to be the training coordinators for the mission. I took some joy, and I admit, pride, when I eventually learned the President Witt could tell no difference between my quality of work and that of the sister who had the position before me whom he had considered the perfect administrative assistant.

Our six month extension finally came to an end. We would have gladly extended again if we were asked, but we were not. Because there is a time and season for all things perhaps even President Witt would not have asked us to extend had he still been the president, but even his time had come to an end and a new president had arrived. President Snow operated differently than President Witt and he decided that he didn't need the missionary couples and many missions ended with his arrival. We went home to our house on the river and took up where we had left off.

Hawaii

For the next three years we did what grandma's and grandpa's do—we hosted family gatherings, we made family visits on special occasions such as graduations and baptisms and baby blessings, and we filled the space in-between with volunteer temple work in the Logan temple. We would travel to Logan twice a week to do this work. The drive was long, but the scenery was beautiful and the work meaningful. And long drives are a pleasant way to spend time with the one you love.

As the year 2000 approached I began feeling antsy. My life was good and blessed, but something was missing. I longed for the fullness I felt when I was serving in the Temple Square Mission. We had the money; we had the time; and we had health so why not go on another mission? When brought this up to Reed he wasn't so sure. He was concerned about the millennium arriving and all the hubbub that the world might fall apart. He was also concerned about our home. On our last mission we had let a family live there and that hadn't worked out so well. He would rather let the house stand empty this time, but that worried him also.

On our temple square mission we had, quite by accident, become closely acquainted with Elder David B. Haight. We had met him in the Church office building cafeteria and he invited us to sit and have lunch with him. Elder Haight grew up in Oakley, Idaho, near where we lived so we found we had several things in common. We had two or three more lunches with Elder Haight during our mission and enjoyed his company very much. Based on this acquaintance, Reed called Elder Haight to discuss his concerns about going on another mission. Elder Haight listened politely, but when Reed had finished he said without hesitation, "Don't give another thought. Go on a mission. The Lord needs you." Elder Haight was over the Missionary Department at the time and told us that when we had our papers ready to send them directly to him.

It can take weeks to take care of all the paperwork required to go on a mission, but when we did we had our final interview with our stake president. Our stake president knew of our correspondence with Elder Haight and said, "Would you like to deliver these papers to him yourself?"

Reed leaned forward and said, "You bet!"

We called Elder Haight's assistant and made an appointment to deliver the papers. On the appointed day we arrived to find Elder Haight needing to leave right away to go to another important meeting that had arisen. It wasn't necessary for Elder Haight to meet with us to deliver our papers and his willingness to do so was pure cordiality in line with the meaning of Charity on his part. Now that another meeting outside of his control had arisen he just wouldn't have the time to meet with us. However, being skilled in the art of kindness and consideration he said, "But walk with me down to my car and we'll talk." Then with a smile he added, "We'll walk slow."

We had a wonderful chat with him and he again reaffirmed that our decision to go on a mission was in accordance to the Lord's will. Just before he got into his car he told us to take our papers back up to his assistant and she would make sure that all was in order. His assistant was a very pleasant lady.

"So, where would you like to go?" she asked. Now this was a real opportunity. She seemed quite sincere in wanting to know as if there might be a good chance to get what we wanted. To this date I don't think many of my family and friends believe me when I tell them our response.

"We will go wherever the Lord wants us to go," we said. That is what was written on our paper in response to the same question.

The assistant laughed and told us she appreciated that. "But you know," she said, "there are only two places that you don't request to go on a mission—those are Hawaii and Nauvoo."

Still, we had no suggestions as to where we wanted to go and left it, "wherever the Lord wants us."

Our call came in record time. Usually it takes ten to fourteen days. We had delivered our papers on a Wednesday and on the following Tuesday we received our call. That was just six days. Reed opened the envelope and read it, but not out loud. I tried to read it over his shoulder, but couldn't see.

"Where are we going?" I said, with just a little emotion.

"You aren't going to believe it," he said, laughing. "Hawaii."

I didn't believe it until I read it for myself. My children can believe this or not, but that is how it happened.

Hawaii is a place that everyone wants to visit and I was no different. I had spent a few days there on a vacation earlier in my life, but now I was going to get to live there for an extended period of time. We were only called for a one year mission, but once again we were asked to extend our mission. President Clark asked us to stay for the duration of his call which was another eleven months. So in the end we were in Hawaii two years.

Over the course of two years we were able to travel around Oahu and see all the usual tourist sites along with many others that tourists miss. However, we were on a mission and a mission requires dedicated work. We worked in the temple six days a week usually for ten hours a day. I would come home exhausted each evening. Temple work doesn't appear to be physically strenuous. You have people who are generally elderly dressed in white suits and dresses—how much strenuous work can you do dressed like that? So why was I so exhausted each night? Too me quite some time to figure it out, but I believe it's because it is takes such focus to perform the temple tasks. Everything in the temple needs to be done perfectly or as perfectly as possible due to the sacred nature of the work. From the moment I entered the temple in the morning to the moment I left in the evening I was in a very focused state of mind and that takes energy.

In the evenings or on our half-day off on Monday we would unwind by visiting the beaches or traveling to see some of the sights with friends. Unlike the young missionaries, we were allowed to go into the ocean at the beaches. I am not a swimmer, but I enjoyed getting some exercise by bouncing in the swells that rolled onto the beach.

We found Hawaii to be very pleasant, not only in weather, but also in culture. We were surrounded by easy going, friendly people both inside and outside the temple. We were honored to be "adopted" into a Hawaiian family, the Au You's and were invited to their family luau. They had invited extended family, some of whom had been BYU football players. We are big BYU football fans and this made it all the more fun.

It was the mission work itself that dominated our days. Most of the temple patrons were local, but we also had many LDS tourists who came to Hawaii for vacation who would take the time to attend the temple. These people came from all over the world and in a day we might hear many different languages.

One group I remember well came from the Marshall Islands. Attending the temple had not been a vacation trip for them. The distance and expense made attending the Hawaiian Temple a once-in-a-lifetime trip. They were not "poor" people, but they did not have much cash flow and had to work hard to put together the funds they needed. One of the men, when I met him, was in a wheel chair. He had been earning money for the trip by diving, without scuba gear, for pearls. I wasn't able to understand the nature of the accident, but it had cost him the use of his legs. I was one of those privileged to attend this group as they went through the temple and see the joy of their dream fulfilled. It was in the Celestial Room that this man in the wheel chair, with great happiness on his face, said to me, "It was worth it!"

Another aspect of temple work that I loved was working with families who had come to be sealed for eternity. Sometimes it was just a young couple just being married. In that case I might be lucky enough to attend to the bride as she prepared for the marriage ceremony. At other times entire families with children would come through to be sealed together if the parents had not originally been married in the temple. Sometimes I would get to help the children as they got dressed in their white clothes and then bring them to the sealing rooms where their parents waited. There are many beautiful sights in the world, but none is more beautiful than seeing a family kneeling around the alter in the temple, holding hands, being sealed together for eternity. Whether it was with a bride or with a family I felt blessed to be able to share such a momentous and memorable event in their lives.

It may be cliché to say it, but still it is the truth, the hardest part of our mission to Hawaii was leaving. We are taught in the gospel that you learn to love the people whom you serve and there are many in Hawaii who hold our hearts to this day. We arrived home in November of 2001 and once again returned to our regular lives as Mom and Dad and Grandma and Grandpa.

Utah

During this stay at home we made a major move in our lives. Reed was an Idaho native and I, although an Iowa transplant, had become an Idahoan at heart after living there for twenty five years. Between us we had raised eleven children in Idaho, none of whom lived there anymore. My children had gone off to school, mainly in Utah, and never come back. Some of Reed's children had done the same. Others had lost the farm in difficult times and moved to Utah to pursue other career opportunities. Reed and I were now living in Idaho all by ourselves. We had gone back to serving as volunteers in Logan Temple and the drive was long. Reed decided that if we were going to continue working in the temple, why didn't we move somewhere nearer a temple? With most of our children living in Utah, Utah is where we put our sights. After a lot of looking everything came together in American Fork. We found a comfortable, but modest home in a gated community that was nearing completion. There was a church across the street, the Timpanogas Temple just up the street, and a WalMart and Costco nearby. It was perfect. On September 18, 2002 we uprooted ourselves from Idaho and replanted ourselves in Utah.

Humanitarian

No sooner had we gotten settled in our new home than the bishop of our new ward called us in. I was certain we were going to receive a calling on a committee or as teachers, but his first words after we sat down were, "I'm calling you on a mission." My heart jumped. Although going on another mission wasn't out of the question in my life I wasn't quite ready to leave my new home. It ended up that we didn't have to leave. We were called to the Church's humanitarian mission. This particular humanitarian mission was located in the local designated humanitarian center that happened to be our stake center. We would be able to come home every night and have most weekends off. This sounded easy and we agreed to the mission. We completed all the paperwork, as usual, and a few weeks later received our nametags and began our mission.

We quickly learned that there was nothing easy about this mission. Where the temple mission wore me out because of the constant focus it took, this mission wore me out because it demanded hard, physical labor. We and two other couples were the foundation of the work. We would set up tables and chairs in the cultural hall in preparation for the volunteers who would come. These tables would serve as assembly lines where we would assemble various humanitarian kits—mainly hygiene kits, school kits, and birthing kits. These hygiene kits had items such as soap, toothpaste and toothbrush, and shampoo. The school kits had paper, erasers, scissors, pencils, slates, chalk, and colored pencils. The birthing kits had a big pad, a clamp, scissors, a blanket and other things helpful to delivering a baby.

The volunteers would put these kits together. The boxes would be sealed and then stacked along the wall. At the end of a session there would be hundreds of boxes forming their own wall. On the days after the volunteers were finished the real work began. We and the other couples would dolly the boxes outside where pallets were waiting. We would stack the boxes about seven feet high in a special formation on the pallets and then wrap them in cellophane. A man with a truck would then come and load the truck with his fork lift and take them away. Then we couples would go back in, take down the tables, put the chairs away, and clean the cultural hall so that it could be used for other purposes. This stacking, and carting, and restacking, and setting up and taking down were exhausting. After these days Reed and I would come home and lay in the hot tub where we would sometimes fall asleep. I told Reed that we were going to drown in the tub some night.

Luckily for us every day didn't involve the assembly lines and the stacking. On other days we would prepare for the assembly lines by gathering together the needed materials. This might involve going to Salt Lake City to pick up boxes, or going to some other storage location to pick up the supplies to go in the kits. Then we would have to prepare the items to be used efficiently in the assembly lines. Some weeks the assembly line locations would be changed so that volunteers in another area could have an opportunity to do the humanitarian work. Like our other missions this mission was a full-time commitment that filled our work week.

I can't remember exactly, but perhaps at first, as I stacked and carted boxes, I may have wondered why I had agreed to do such mundane, hard work when I could be relaxing on my patio and taking care of my tomatoes. If I did ever wonder the wonder was swept away with enjoyable associations with volunteers who, too, got caught up in the wonderful spirit of the work. These volunteers were, more often than not, strangers to me, but strangers who, for the day, became brothers and sisters in serving those in the world who truly needed a hand. Although they focused and worked hard there was a peace and happiness about them that they may not have felt when they arrived. Where they experienced this the one time they volunteered I was blessed to experience this week after week.

Sister Gunther, who headed up this humanitarian mission, once had a man come in to speak to us. This man was often on the delivery end of mission. He had made deliveries in countries around the world and told how well-received the kits were. Often there were tears of joy. There was nothing grand in these boxes, but it was often something they had never owned before and something that was truly useful. He said he saw children breaking the bright yellow pencils in two in order to share them with a sibling or a friend. He ran into an LDS soldier who had just returned from a mission far out in the mountains of Afghanistan. This soldier said that in some non-descript village that he might not even be able to find again he saw a Church humanitarian kit that probably had been put together in our stake center in American Fork, Utah. The work was very hard and held no glamour or recognition, but knowing that the work did make a positive difference in the world left us gratified.

We had not been called on this mission for a specific period of time and it looked like it may have gone on indefinitely. It came to an unceremonious end after two years when Reed needed emergency open-heart surgery. Reed eventually recovered from the ordeal, but that ended our humanitarian mission.

Washington DC

Eleven months after Reed's surgery my sister Dorothy and her husband, Robert, were visiting us. The topic of missions came up. We hadn't been considering another mission at the time, but Bob and Dorty had been tossing the idea around. They had pretty much decided against it for fear of not knowing where they might end up serving. We mentioned to them that any more couples actually had a choice of places they could serve. A few days after they had returned home I got a call from Bob. He had been looking at mission possibilities and one had caught his eye.

"If we went to the Washington DC Temple Mission would you two come with us?"

"Maybe we would," I said. "Let me talk to my bishop."

Our bishop made some calls and told us that the Washington DC Temple president asked if we could start tomorrow. They needed people that badly.

On 2005 Bob and Dort and Reed and I loaded up our vehicles and drove across the country to Washington DC. We found neighboring apartments and moved in. The work in the temple was the same as in Hawaii with the same long hours and the same wonderful joys. This time, though, I also found myself doing dishes in the cafeteria, folding laundry, and other general cleaning duties. I didn't mind these duties as the sweet spirit of the Lord filled every room of the temple.

Outside the temple I didn't find life nearly as enjoyable as Hawaii. The streets were narrow and crowded and the people weren't nearly as friendly. There were so many trees and the land was so flat that I couldn't see the horizon or any sunsets. There certainly is nothing wrong with Washington DC, but the differences in geography and lifestyle sometimes challenged my attitude. In spite of my dislike of Washington DC life in general we had a wonderful mission experience in the Washington DC Temple. It was particularly memorable because of all the time I was able to spend with my sister and brother-in-law. In our off hours we were able to visit all the historic sites out there and we made a lot of memories together. At the end of our one year commitment, in 2006, we returned to Utah.

An Unpleasant Break

For two years we lived the more regular lives of a retired couple although we did serve two part time church service missions two or more days a week giving tours and ushering at the Church Conference Center and serving in the Mt. Timpanogos Temple. During these two years life threw me a change-up. For several years I had been suffering from pain in my hips. This pain had been growing worse each year. After consulting with a doctor I made the decision to get my hips replaced. These replacements would be done one at a time with recovery time in-between. The first replacement went very well, but I do remember the pain during recovery being so bad that it made me wonder if I had done the right thing. It was after this first hip replacement that the complication arose. Ironically, the complication had nothing to do with the hip replacement surgery. After I had recovered from the first hip replacement I went to a doctor about another problem. He told me after the initial examination that he was certain that it was nothing. But the next day I received a call from him.

"I'm afraid I was totally wrong on this one," he said.

"Oh?" I said, a cold feeling growing in my stomach.

"The tests show that your kidney is most likely full of cancer."

I had been a nurse for 30 years and had seen the most horrible medical conditions. I had seen children die horribly from burns in my emergency room one day, but had always been able to come back to work the next day and move on in a professional manner. My training and experience didn't help here. I don't think any normal human being can be told they have a malignant cancer in their body and not suddenly feel a little dizzy.

"As far as cancer goes," the doctor went on, "I feel good about this one. I have reason to believe it hasn't spread. We have a good chance of stopping it"

I was glad to hear his opinion, but where he had been wrong to begin with my fear was still great.

I was already scheduled for my second hip replacement, but clearly I needed to get the cancerous kidney removed first. I didn't tell my hip doctor about my kidney removal because I was afraid they would cancel the surgery. I knew if they cancelled it would be months and months before they could reschedule. I didn't want to put up with the pain that long. They removed my kidney and I awoke to the good news that they had found no sign that the cancer had spread. The doctor believed they had got it all. I was very grateful for this news and could start planning again for years in the future. Three weeks later I had my second hip replacement.

Family History

A year later, although I was a little slower getting up and down, I was still cancer free and feeling pretty good. There was still much talk of how much couples were needed to fill position all over the world. I looked at myself and at Reed. We were still healthy and financially able. What excuses could I give the Lord about why we didn't use our health and means in his service? I spoke with a long-time friend who was serving a mission in the Family and Church History mission. I found out that there were twenty-eight different zones in this mission, each area responsible for something totally different than the others. My friend told me they desperately needed help in this mission. It was a full-time mission, but we would be allowed to live at home and drive up to downtown Salt Lake City every morning. This attracted me and Reed was willing. We, for the fifth time, went through all the paper work and requested the Family History Mission. Waiting for our call was still exciting because we did not know to which one of the twenty-two areas in the mission we would be called. Our call came and we were called to work in the conservation lab, a place we didn't even know existed. We would start August 2009 and work behind the scenes in the Churches main Family History Center across West Temple from Temple Square.

This mission was much more difficult at first than the others. We were working side-by-side with professionals—staff who had been doing the work for years. The work was very technical and was expected to be done at a professional level. Reed found himself binding books. He discovered how much focus and work it took to put a high quality, hard-back cover on a book. He also discovered the embarrassment of finishing a book binding only to find out it was on upside-down. He experienced this more than once.

Among other things I found myself taking family history books apart and then preparing them to be put back together again. There were many technical details I had to learn and follow and I found it frustrating at first. But as time went on I got better and better at it and found it very fulfilling. I told my children more than once that I couldn't believe I was able to do the technical work I was doing. I had been a surgeon's assistant, an emergency room nurse, and an EMT, but this work was so different I couldn't help but feel proud for learning how to do it so well.

The most difficult part of this work ended up being the daily drive from American Fork to downtown Salt Lake. The traffic was always so heavy on good days and then there was always construction to make it worse. We had to arise at 4:00 am in order to get ready and arrive on time. The work was very physical for both of us and we came home exhausted. I've learned that being exhausted for good reason is a good thing.

We worked in the mission for the duration of our one-year commitment. In August of 2010 our Church History mission came to an end. This mission was even more short-handed when we left than when we began. They made it known they would be very happy if we stayed on. We were both tired, however, and nearing eighty-years-old. We needed a break.

The End (or Not)

At the writing of this book the Family History Mission was our last mission. It very well could be that we will never go on another full-time mission. Maybe I just haven't had enough time to recover from the hard work of the Family History Mission and so another full-time mission isn't yet appealing. It could be that I am just wearing down. At the moment staying home and receiving visits from and making visits to our children and grandchildren sounds pretty good. Even if I like the idea of staying around home, I find myself with plenty of energy to share.

I have discovered "indexing." Using an on-line program I am able to enter family history information into a database maintained by the Church where it is made accessible to anyone in the world who is interested in his or her family tree. The truth is, I find this activity addicting. I will sit down and planning on indexing for an hour only to find myself still there four hours later. This is important work for humanity and I feel it is a mission even if not official. When I am not indexing you might find me shouting at the TV during a BYU football game or when watching the Jazz come back from a double-digit deficit. I might be going to the Mormon Tabernacle Choir Christmas program with guest David Archuleta. There is a very good chance you will find me making out birthday cards to one of my five children, six step-children, or 65 grandchildren and great-grandchildren. On the other hand Reed and I are not averse to going on a cruise as we have done before. I come from a long-lived family. I know that today could be my last, or I might be around another decade or more. Either way I would not feel cheated.

Epilogue

While bringing in cows from their summer pasture on that Iowa farm of my girlhood I would sing. I couldn't have put words as to why I sang then, but now I can; I sang because I had dreams for the future. My dreams weren't clear to me then. They were just a good feeling born of some unknown hope. If a window suddenly opened in the shimmering summer air and that young girl saw me sitting on the couch where I sit now she would not recognize herself. She would only see an old woman. I wonder, though, if she might take a second look and wonder at something familiar in my eyes. Oh, but I would recognize her. When she, bare footed, stepped in that cow patty because she wasn't paying attention I would just laugh. "Yes, that's right, Laurie," I would say as she grimaced and grumbled. "Just wipe it off as best you can and keep going. A little cow patty between the toes won't keep you from singing."

Reed and I during our mission at the Hawaii Temple in 2001. Pictures like this sure bring back many happy memories of our time in Hawaii.

www.ingramcontent.com/pod-product-compliance
Lightning Source LLC
Chambersburg PA
CBHW020307290526
45784CB00003B/1392